If we had told people we were going to build a new bug tracker, they would have told us we were completely nuts. A little research into the market would tell you that there are scores, maybe hundreds, of potential competitors, from mega-expensive corporate systems and free open source projects, to on-demand software-as-a-service applications and homegrown tools purpose built to do one thing and do it well. And then there's Microsoft Excel, the all-in-one list builder and charting tool, which is still incredibly popular among small software teams.

Had we considered the massive competition out there, we may have never created JIRA. Fortunately for us, we had some naïveté in our favour, and no one told us *not* to do it. We built JIRA to help us track our own consulting business, which is what Atlassian was in 2001, and in 2002 it became a full-fledged product.

There's two reasons JIRA was successful: an unexpected business model and its flexible architecture. In 2002, Atlassian's sales model was unlike any other business-to-business software tools. It wasn't free like an open source project, but it wasn't expensive either like products from big corporations. It didn't require any professional services to use. And there were no sales people. It caused some confusion in the market. *Can you help us set up an evaluation?* Um, just download it and try it. *How can we make changes to the license agreement?* You can't. It's one size fits all. *How much for a support agreement?* It's included. Free. *Can I send you a purchase order?* Sure, or you can use your credit card. *A credit card? To purchase enterprise software?*

Of course, JIRA's popularity is more than a price point and business model. Most of the developers who started working on JIRA in 2003 are still at Atlassian today, building atop one of the most feature-rich and flexible issue trackers available. Depending on which company is using it, JIRA has been called a bug tracker, issue tracker, defect tracker, task tracker, project management system, or help desk system. It's used by waterfall and agile development teams. It's used by some of the largest corporations in the world to help build their biggest products, and some people use it to manage their personal cross country moves. The permissions system has allowed JIRA to work for both private and public-facing projects.

An ecosystem has been built up around JIRA. As of the time of writing this foreword, there are 273 commercial and open source plugins to JIRA on the Atlassian Plugin Exchange, and hundreds of other integrations built by companies for in-house use or by vendors who sell complementary products. We're extremely excited for Matt's book, too. Matt has been a terrific partner who has built custom integrations for JIRA, extending it far and beyond. In some ways, this book is another plugin to JIRA, helping customers to squeeze more value from the application. It's sure to provide assistance to all the aforementioned customers—the big companies and the small ones, the ones looking to configure it as a bug tracker, and those looking for project management tool.

The final word is about our customers who have pushed the product, our product and support teams, and our imaginations, further then we could have ever done by ourselves. It's been a lot of fun, and for that, we say *thanks, mate.*

Mike Cannon-Brookes and Scott Farquhar, Atlassian co-founders and CEOs

Practical JIRA Plugins

Matthew B. Doar

Beijing · Cambridge · Farnham · Köln · Sebastopol · Tokyo

Practical JIRA Plugins
by Matthew B. Doar

Copyright © 2012 Matthew B. Doar. All rights reserved.
Printed in the United States of America.

Published by O'Reilly Media, Inc., 1005 Gravenstein Highway North, Sebastopol, CA 95472.

O'Reilly books may be purchased for educational, business, or sales promotional use. Online editions are also available for most titles (*http://my.safaribooksonline.com*). For more information, contact our corporate/institutional sales department: (800) 998-9938 or *corporate@oreilly.com*.

Editors: Mike Loukides and Meghan Blanchette	**Cover Designer:** Karen Montgomery
Production Editor: Kristen Borg	**Interior Designer:** David Futato
Proofreader: O'Reilly Production Services	**Illustrator:** Robert Romano

July 2011:   First Edition.

Revision History for the First Edition:
2011-07-22   First release
2012-09-01   Second release
See *http://oreilly.com/catalog/errata.csp?isbn=9781449308278* for release details.

ISBN: 978-1-449-30827-8

[LSI]

1346366395

Table of Contents

Preface

What This Book Is About

This book is about plugins for *JIRA*, the popular issue tracker from *Atlassian*. An issue tracker lets people collaborate better when there are things to be done. You can use an issue tracker for everything from tracking bugs in software, to customer support requests, and beyond. Plugins extend what JIRA can do and can be developed separately from JIRA. Plugins are a specific kind of "add-ons" that need to be installed in JIRA server. Other add-ons are integrations or client-side scripts.

This book is intended for people who want to create and maintain JIRA plugins. Plugins have been a part of JIRA since version 3.0 and a significant community has emerged around them. That community is even large enough to have an annual gathering known as *AtlasCamp*.

Writing JIRA plugins requires some technical knowledge. This book assumes that you can write simple Java program and are familiar with ideas such as implementing an interface, extending a class and where to find information about the core Java classes. In a few places this book also assumes that you have access to the JIRA source code. This is available from Atlassian with any JIRA license that costs $10 or more.

The intention of this book is to supplement but not repeat the extensive JIRA documentation freely available at *http://confluence.atlassian.com/display/JIRA/JIRA+Docu mentation*. Most of the chapters in this book depend upon information in Chapter 1, but can otherwise be read in any order. This book is a companion to *Practical JIRA Administration* (O'Reilly).

In selecting the different plugins to cover in this book, I was conscious of the different kinds of JIRA plugins that I am asked to implement most frequently as a software toolsmith. I chose the most commonly requested ones. If you can't find a particular plugin type and think it should be in this book, then please do contact me with more details.

JIRA Versions and System Details

The first edition of this book referred to JIRA version *4.2.4 Standalone* which was released in February 2011. This is the second edition and refers to version *5.1.2* which was released in August 2012. Where there are differences between versions of JIRA (or for JIRA OnDemand/Studio or JIRA WAR/EAR), these are noted in the text.

The target system used throughout this book is a Linux server with JDK 1.6 and MySQL. The main differences for other operating systems, deployment types, databases, and JVMs are the installation instructions and the names and paths of certain files. These details are described in the online JIRA documentation.

Development Environment

This book was written using OSX 10.7.3 on a Mac Mini Server using DocBook 4.5, Emacs 22.1.50.1 and Subversion 1.6.7. The output files were generated using a custom remote toolchain provided by O'Reilly for their authors. Using a remote toolchain makes it easier to use DocBook and allows books to be updated more frequently.

Technical Reviewers

Jamie Echlin
> Jamie has been using the Atlassian tools since 2006, and is the author of several popular JIRA plugins.

David Fischer
> David is a seasoned CTO who, since he discovered JIRA in 2004, never used another issue tracker again. He is also the founder of Innovalog, a consulting firm specializing in software industrialization, and the developer of the popular JIRA Misc Workflow Extensions Jira plugin.

John Kodumal
> John is a Technical Lead at Atlassian.

Conventions Used in This Book

The following typographical conventions are used in this book:

Italic
> Indicates new terms, URLs, email addresses, filenames, and file extensions.

`Constant width`
> Used for program listings, as well as within paragraphs to refer to program elements such as variable or function names, databases, data types, environment variables, statements, and keywords.

`Constant width bold`
> Shows commands or other text that should be typed literally by the user.

Constant width italic
> Shows text that should be replaced with user-supplied values or by values determined by context.

Administration→System→System Information
> Shows menu selections within JIRA, in this case the Administration menu item, the System menu item and then the System Information menu item.

This icon signifies a tip, suggestion, or general note.

This icon indicates a warning or caution.

Using Code Examples

The source code for all the examples in this book is available from *https://marketplace .atlassian.com/41293*.

This book is here to help you get your job done. In general, you may use the code in this book in your programs and documentation. You do not need to contact us for permission unless you're reproducing a significant portion of the code. For example, writing a program that uses several chunks of code from this book does not require permission. Selling or distributing a CD-ROM of examples from O'Reilly books does require permission. Answering a question by citing this book and quoting example code does not require permission. Incorporating a significant amount of example code from this book into your product's documentation does require permission.

We appreciate, but do not require, attribution. An attribution usually includes the title, author, publisher, and ISBN. For example: "*Practical JIRA Plugins* by Matthew B. Doar (O'Reilly). Copyright 2012 O'Reilly Media, 978-1-449-30827-8."

If you feel your use of code examples falls outside fair use or the permission given above, feel free to contact us at *permissions@oreilly.com*.

Safari® Books Online

Safari Books Online is an on-demand digital library that lets you easily search over 7,500 technology and creative reference books and videos to find the answers you need quickly.

With a subscription, you can read any page and watch any video from our library online. Read books on your cell phone and mobile devices. Access new titles before they are available for print, and get exclusive access to manuscripts in development and post feedback for the authors. Copy and paste code samples, organize your favorites, download chapters, bookmark key sections, create notes, print out pages, and benefit from tons of other time-saving features.

O'Reilly Media has uploaded this book to the Safari Books Online service. To have full digital access to this book and others on similar topics from O'Reilly and other publishers, sign up for free at *http://my.safaribooksonline.com*.

How to Contact Us

Please address comments and questions concerning this book to the publisher:

> O'Reilly Media, Inc.
> 1005 Gravenstein Highway North
> Sebastopol, CA 95472
> 800-998-9938 (in the United States or Canada)
> 707-829-0515 (international or local)
> 707-829-0104 (fax)

We have a web page for this book, where we list errata, examples, and any additional information. You can access this page at:

> *http://www.oreilly.com/catalog/9781449308278*

To comment or ask technical questions about this book, send email to:

> *bookquestions@oreilly.com*

For more information about our books, courses, conferences, and news, see our website at *http://www.oreilly.com*.

Find us on Facebook: *http://facebook.com/oreilly*

Follow us on Twitter: *http://twitter.com/oreillymedia*

Watch us on YouTube: *http://www.youtube.com/oreillymedia*

Content Updates

September 2012

The complete list of changes in each release of JIRA can be seen at *http://confluence .atlassian.com/display/JIRA/Production+Releases*. The changes to JIRA that are related to the content of this book include the following:

- A major change in JIRA 5.0 was the definition of a public, supported Java API. This means that plugins developed for one version of JIRA using the public API should continue to work with newer versions of JIRA. This promises to reduce the overhead of maintaining JIRA plugins.

- The Atlassian Developer Toolbox gives plugin developers a single place to go for useful tools such as the REST API browser, the Plugin Checkup tool and more.
- The Plugin SDK has made creating skeleton plugins easier, and deploying changes is now much faster in many cases.
- The release of still more open source plugins by the Atlassian team has provided many more examples for plugin developers to use for their own plugins.
- The tutorials and other developer documentation for JIRA has seen significant improvement, both in quantity and quality.

Acknowledgments

Many people at Atlassian have encouraged and assisted me with this book, but Bryan Rollins, Andreas Knecht, Jonathan Doklovic, and Dan Rosen stand out. Ben Speakmon has written many of the better tutorials that are now available. Thanks also to my colleagues and clients at CustomWare, past and present. But in the end it's the Atlassian developer community that makes it worth writing a book like this. Thank you to all of you for your generously given information and intriguing discussions over the past five years.

My sincere thanks also go to all the clients of Consulting Toolsmiths for directly and indirectly providing me with the knowledge of which JIRA plugins are hardest to get right.

Behind all I do is my dearest wife Katherine and beloved children Lizi, Jacob, and Luke. Thank you all, and may the love of God rest and remain with you always.

## CHAPTER 1

Plugin Basics

Overview

Building any plugin for JIRA starts with downloading the most recent Atlassian Plugin SDK (Software Development Kit) from the Atlassian Developers site at *https://developer .atlassian.com/display/DOCS/Set+up+the+Atlassian+Plugin+SDK+and+Build+a +Project*.[1] This chapter explains how to use the Plugin SDK and some other things common to all plugins. The same SDK is also used to develop plugins for other Atlassian products such as *Confluence*. Subsequent chapters contain details about specific kinds of JIRA plugins.

If you haven't already found them, there are a number of tutorials about developing different kinds of plugins online at *https://developer.atlassian.com/display/JIRADEV/ JIRA+Plugin+Tutorials*. I recommend using them and their source code at *https://bit bucket.org/atlassian_tutorial*along with this book since they mostly complement each other.

The Atlassian Answers site at *http://answers.atlassian.com* is the best place to ask technical questions about how to develop plugins. The tag "jira-development" is most commonly used. The old JIRA Developer Forum at *http://forums.atlassian.com/forum .jspa?forumID=100* is also a useful place to find answers but it's now read-only.

Beyond some basic Java skills, in order to write a JIRA plugin you'll also need to understand how Apache Velocity templates are used by JIRA. These are the files that control how HTML pages are formatted, and are covered in more detail in "Apache Velocity" on page 12. For more complicated plugins you may need to know more about Apache Maven, the build and deploy tool for Java described in the section "Maven" on page 14.

JIRA uses many other technologies and it can be useful to have some familiarity with any of these: Subversion, Mercurial, Ant, Apache JSP, JavaScript, JQuery, Soy and

---

1. This SDK is not the same as the old "JIRA Plugin Development Kit", which was used for JIRA 3.x plugins.

Jersey for REST. However for most plugins you won't need to know anything about them—just Java and a bit of Velocity and Maven.

Creating a JIRA Plugin

JIRA plugins use an Apache Maven 2 project for each plugin to produce a Java `.jar` file that can be installed in JIRA.

A Maven project has a fairly rigid layout, always with a top-level XML file named *pom.xml* made up of the plugin's name, version, dependencies and so on. The `groupId` and `artifactId` variables in *pom.xml* are what make a plugin unique within Maven. The `artifactId` is also what will appear as part of your plugin .jar file's name. The `name` variable is the more verbose name of the plugin, as seen in the JIRA plugin administration pages. The SDK will create a working *pom.xml* file for us with some reasonable default values.

 Atlassian's guidelines on the use of "JIRA" are that a name such as "Acme plugin for JIRA®" is okay, whereas "JIRA® plugin for Acme" is not. The former connotes a 3rd party plugin for JIRA®, while the latter connotes an Atlassian-developed tool. More information is available at *http://www.atlassian.com/company/trademark* or contact *developer-relations@atlassian.com*.

The first thing to do is to unpack the SDK in a convenient location. This location is referred to as $SDK_HOME in the examples below. You can then create a JIRA plugin with a single command:

```
$SDK_HOME/bin/atlas-create-jira-plugin
```

This command will prompt you for a few values and then create a new plugin directory with enough files to build a plugin. This skeleton plugin does nothing, but it can be installed in JIRA and will appear in the list of plugins shown in the Administration plugins page.

As mentioned earlier, the `artifactId` and `groupId` values appear directly in the Maven *pom.xml* file. Every Atlassian plugin has a unique identifier named *key*. The key for each plugin is defined in the file *atlassian-plugin.xml*, and by default the key is "artifactId.groupId".

The `version` argument is the version of your plugin, not the JIRA version. Versions can be any text but the Atlassian Marketplace (see the section "Atlassian Marketplace" on page 85) now requires that the version starts with three sets of digits, not two. A version can also look like `5.1.0-alpha`. The `package` argument is the name of the Java package that the plugin's Java source code will use.

If you want to, you can also provide the same information that was required to create a plugin directly from the command line:

```
$SDK_HOME/bin/atlas-create-jira-plugin \
  --artifactId myplugin \
  --groupId com.mycompany.jira.plugins \
  --version 5.1.0 \
  --package com.mycompany.jira.plugins.myplugin
  --non-interactive
```

Important Plugin Files

The most important files in a plugin directory and their purposes are as follows.

pom.xml
: The top-level Maven 2 project file for the plugin.

README
: The place to start for the description of what the plugin is intended to do. This can be renamed to anything you like or removed.

LICENSE
: A place holder for the license for the plugin. Many JIRA plugins use the BSD license by default, but the section "Further Reading" on page 15 has more information about choosing a license.

src
: The directory that contains all the source files needed to build the plugin.

src/main/resources/atlassian-plugin.xml
: The XML file that specifies exactly what the plugin really contains. The order of the elements in this file doesn't make a difference to how they work.

src/main/java/com/mycompany/jira/plugins/myplugin
: The default location for Java source files, based on the **package** name used when the plugin was created.

src/main/java/com/mycompany/jira/plugins/myplugin/MyPlugin.java
: A sample Java source file, automatically generated. You can rename or delete this file later on.

target
: The location of all generated files after a build has finished. None of the files in this directory need to be version controlled.

target/myplugin-5.1.0.jar
: The generated plugin package that is deployed to JIRA to actually use the plugin. The filename contains the version that was specified in *pom.xml*.

There are a few other files generated in the *src/test* directory related to testing your plugin. You can delete them if they're not wanted, but an even better practice is to write some tests as described at *https://developer.atlassian.com/display/DOCS/Plugin+Test ing+Resources+and+Discussion.*

Reading a Plugin

Before diving into building a plugin, it's useful to know how to understand what any JIRA plugin does. Knowing how to read a plugin also makes it easier to find examples on which to base your own work.

My own approach is to start with the top-level Maven file *pom.xml* and to look for the `jira.version` element. That should tell you which version of JIRA the plugin was last built against. If it's too old for you to use, then see "Updating a Plugin Version at the Marketplace" on page 89 for ideas on how to update it. There is also a `jira.data.ver sion` element that tells you the version of the JIRA database schema the plugin last worked with. As might be expected, this changes less frequently than `jira.version` but should be close to the value of `jira.version`.

The next file to read is *src/main/resources/atlassian-plugin.xml*. This file contains all the different plugin module types that are used in the plugin and tells you what the plugin provides; e.g., a new custom field type. The initial skeleton plugin doesn't have any plugin modules in this file because it doesn't do anything.

Then I'll read any documentation or perhaps look at a few screen shots. Usually only after all that do I look at actual Java source code and Velocity template files.

Building and Deploying a Plugin

The minimal commands to build a plugin from the command line are:

```
$ cd myplugin
$ $SDK_HOME/bin/atlas-package
...
[INFO] ----------------------------------------------------
[INFO] BUILD SUCCESSFUL
[INFO] ----------------------------------------------------
[INFO] Total time: 26 seconds
[INFO] Finished at: Wed May 11 03:11:48 PDT 2011
[INFO] Final Memory: 56M/118M
[INFO] ----------------------------------------------------
```

This last command will download the dependencies listed in the *pom.xml*, which includes the large `atlassian-jira-N.N.N.jar` for the version of JIRA specified in `jira.version` in *pom.xml*. Before spending time downloading these large files, it's worth checking that the `jira.version` is set to the version of JIRA you really want to use.

The command will then compile the Java source files and create the plugin's .jar file. You should make sure that you have a recent Java JDK installed on the machine where the plugin is being built. JIRA 4.1 supports the Oracle (formerly Sun) JDK 1.5, but JIRA 4.2 and later require JDK 1.6. JIRA 5.1 does not support JDK 1.7.

The first time all this is done it can take a while but subsequently should be faster. If the dependencies in your *pom.xml* file don't change, then you can even add the `-o` or `--offline` flag to *atlas-package* to work offline and make the build a little faster.

When the build is finished you should see a `.jar` file in the *target* directory. That's your plugin .jar file.

To deploy the plugin to a production JIRA instance, copy the plugin .jar file to *plugins/ installed-plugins* in the `JIRA_HOME` directory—or with JIRA 4.3 and later, you can upload it using Administration→Plugins and the *Install* or *Manage Plugins* tab. Prior to JIRA 4.4, most JIRA plugins require you to restart JIRA to complete a plugin installation or update.

Using atlas-run and atlas-cli

The SDK also provides another way to build and deploy a JIRA plugin. If you type:

```
$SDK_HOME/bin/atlas-run
```

instead of *atlas-package*, then a brand new instance of JIRA is automatically configured in the *target* directory. Then the plugin .jar file is deployed there and the new JIRA instance is started up at `http://localhost:2990/jira`. You can log in with the user name `admin` and password `admin` and test your plugin directly there.

This second approach takes a little longer to start up the first time, but you don't have to configure anything such as a license. The other benefit of this approach is that in some cases it allows for much faster redeployment of plugins. If you open another separate window from the same top-level directory and type:

```
$SDK_HOME/bin/atlas-cli
```

then a `maven2>` prompt appears. Typing `pi` for "plugin install" at the prompt will rebuild and redeploy your plugin in a few seconds instead of the minute or so it can take to restart JIRA. More information about all of the SDK commands can be found at *https: //developer.atlassian.com/display/DOCS/Atlassian+Plugin+SDK+Commands*

This is a fast way to develop plugins, but prior to JIRA 4.4, it only works if a plugin is using certain plugin module types. The list of which types do and do not work with `pi` can be found at *https://developer.atlassian.com/display/DOCS/Plugins+that+Cannot +be+Reloaded+with+FastDev+or+pi*. The good news is that as of JIRA 4.4 almost all plugins can be reloaded using `pi` or from the Administration menu, which will save everyone a lot of time during development.

The fastest way to develop a plugin now is to use the FastDev tool (*https://developer .atlassian.com/display/DOCS/Automatic+Plugin+Reinstallation+with+FastDev*). After starting JIRA using the *atlas-cli* command this tool checks each time that a page is reloaded whether the plugin needs to be rebuilt and also reloaded.

What Can JIRA Plugins Do?

Doing something useful in your plugin involves adding one or more plugin modules to the *atlassian-plugin.xml* file. You'll also most likely need to add some Java source and Velocity template files. Chapter 2 and the rest of this book covers exactly how to do that.

There are over 30 different types of plugin modules listed at *http://confluence.atlassian .com/display/JIRA/JIRA+Plugin+Guide*. Each plugin module has a separate page documenting the XML attributes and elements that it supports.

 Much of JIRA's own functionality is defined using these same plugin module types in files with names that look like "system-*-plugin.xml". These source code files are always a good place to check for working examples of each plugin module type. The complete list of JIRA's plugin module types is configured in the file *JiraModuleDescriptorFactory.java*.

The different plugin modules that are documented at *https://developer.atlassian.com/ display/JIRADEV/JIRA+Plugin+Guide* can be grouped as follows.

Custom Fields

customfield-type
> Provides a new type of custom field for JIRA, as described in Chapter 2.

customfield-searcher
> Provides a new searcher for custom fields, described further in Chapter 4.

Workflow

workflow-condition
> Adds a new workflow condition to restrict when the status of an issue is changed. There is an example in "Conditions" on page 63.

workflow-validator
> Adds a new workflow condition to validate the inputs when the status of an issue can be changed. There is an example in "Validators" on page 70.

workflow-function
> Adds a new workflow post-function to update an issue after its status has changed. There is an example of this in "Post-Functions" on page 72.

User Interface

project-tabpanel
component-tabpanel
version-tabpanel
issue-tabpanel
> These plugin modules let you add new tabs to the *Project* page, a project's *Components* page, a project's *Versions* page and to the view screen of an issue.

web-item
web-section
web-panel-renderer
> Add new operations or groups of links to existing JIRA web pages and their menus. Since JIRA 5.0 the renderer module gives you more control over how the content of different parts of JIRA web pages are displayed.

keyboard-shortcut
> Add a new keyboard shortcut to JIRA.

issue-link-renderer
> Change how an remote issue link is displayed. New in JIRA 5.0.

webwork
> Add a new URL and web page to JIRA. This is used as part of the example in "Adding Configuration to a Custom Field" on page 29.

issue-operation
> Prior to JIRA 4.0 this added a new operation to the screen that is shown when viewing an issue. Since replaced by the web-item plugin module

Reporting

gadget
> A new gadget that can be added to a JIRA dashboard.

report
> A report that can be selected from a projects *Project* page.

jqlfunction
> Add a new JIRA Query Language (JQL) function. JQL is mentioned briefly in "How Searchers Work" on page 48.

search-request-view
> Search Request views are the choices of how to view the list of issues in the Issue Navigator; e.g., Printable, Word or Excel.

portlet
> This has been deprecated since JIRA 4.0, when it was replaced by gadgets. It was removed in JIRA 5.0.

Remote Access

rest
> Define a new REST endpoint. REST is the future direction for remote access to JIRA.

rpc-soap
> Add a new SOAP endpoint for JIRA remote access. SOAP is currently the most common way of accessing JIRA remotely.

rpc-xmlrpc
> Add a new XML-RPC endpoint for remote access. This method of accessing JIRA is less frequently used.

Other Plugin Module Types

Some plugin module types are common to all Atlassian plugins. Most of these are documented further at *https://developer.atlassian.com/display/PLUGINFRAME WORK/Plugin+Module+Types*.

resource
web-resource
web-resource-transformer
> These module types refer to other files and resources used by JIRA plugins. Examples include JavaScript and CSS files, image files and internationalization files ("Internationalization" on page 92). Since JIRA 5.0 the transformer module gives you more control over how these files are used in a plugin at runtime.

component
component-import
> These modules are how JIRA defines which classes can be injected into the constructors of the Java classes used within a plugin. They have nothing to do with a project's components.

servlet
servlet-context-listener
servlet-context-param
servlet-filter
> These modules allow you to intercept calls to JIRA URLs and change what is returned, as well as using new Java servlets.

listener
> This module lets you define a listener as part of an Atlassian plugin. More information can be found at *https://developer.atlassian.com/display/CONFDEV/Event +Listener+Module*. Since JIRA 5.0.

module-type
> This module lets you extend the JIRA plugin framework by defining new module types.

user-format
> These let you change how a user's details appear in their profile.

jira-footer
> This undocumented module controls what appears at the bottom of every page in JIRA. An example of its use can be found in the JIRA source file *system-footer-plugin.xml*.

Which Methods Should My Plugin Use?

A public Java API was introduced in JIRA 5.0 (*http://blogs.atlassian.com/2012/03/stable-apis-yes-we-have-them/*). The classes and methods in the public API should not change as rapidly in each minor release. So if your plugin only uses the public API you shouldn't have to update or recompile. A plugin built for JIRA 5.1 should just work when JIRA 5.2 is released. Obviously this promises to save everyone a lot of work. The rest of the core JIRA API is still available for plugins to use, but with the warning that it changes more rapidly that the public API.

To encourage plugin developers to use the public API, Atlassian have created a tool where you can upload a plugin's `.jar` file and see a report about which parts of the plugin are not using the public API for a particular version of JIRA. More information about the plugin checkup tool see *https://developer.atlassian.com/display/CHECKUP/Overview+of+the+Atlassian+Plugin+Checkup*.

The official policy about what will and will not change in the different kinds of releases can be found at *https://developer.atlassian.com/display/JIRADEV/Java+API+Policy+for+JIRA*.

Troubleshooting a Build

In theory building your plugin should just work. In practice you may have one of the following common errors.[2]

If the build fails with the error `Cannot execute mojo: resources` then check that you're in the same directory as the *pom.xml* file.

If you get errors about missing dependencies it means that Maven didn't know how to download a particular file that was specified in a `dependency` element in *pom.xml*. Check for typos in the `groupId` and `artifactId` elements of the `dependency`, particularly if you added them by hand. You may also want to check for newer versions of the same dependency using Google. A few files such as *activation.jar* are not available from a Maven repository due to licensing restrictions, so they have to be downloaded and installed locally if needed.

---

2. "In theory, practice is the same as theory. In practice, it differs." — Yogi Berra

Maven nicely provides you with the necessary command to install a .jar file locally to resolve a missing dependency. If you do this, then don't forget to note where the .jar file was originally downloaded from.

Finding the correct version number for a Maven dependency is not always easy. Sometimes the version can be found by searching for an `artifactId` value in the *pom.xml* files within the JIRA source for the appropriate version of JIRA, or by looking at the version of the different .jar files that are shipped with JIRA. Since JIRA 5.0 the Atlassian Developer Toolbox has a page that shows the component versions being used in an instance of JIRA.

 One useful tip is that any flags after an SDK command are passed directly to Maven. So you can add a parameter such as `--file other-pom.xml` to any *atlas-* command to try debugging a build by using an alternative *pom.xml* file.

Sometimes a build fails when it is building or running unit tests. Those tests are there for a good reason, but if you *really* have to build without them then you can disable them. Adding the parameter `-Dmaven.test.skip` to `$SDK_HOME/bin/atlas-package` prevents Maven from compiling and executing the tests. Or you can skip just their execution with the `-DskipTests` parameter.

It's a good idea to avoid using the `com.atlassian.jira` namespace for your plugin's Java source code. The classes that you create should be only visible to your plugin at runtime, but it's confusing for other people trying to understand your code and is not recommended.

Another thing to be careful about is making sure that you only have one instance of a plugin deployed. Multiple versions of a plugin can accidentally get deployed if you change the plugin's version number and then forget to remove the old plugin .jar file when you deploy the new one. Or if you have deployed a plugin both manually and using JIRA's own plugin manager. Which of the two .jar files is used by JIRA is not defined and unexpected results may occur.

One of the most common problems with JIRA plugins happens at runtime. The log file contains an `UnsatisfiedDependencyException` error about a constructor in your plugin. This and other runtime problems are described in more detail at. *https://developer.at lassian.com/display/DOCS/Plugin+and+Gadget+Gotchas*.

Another runtime error that can be hard to debug is using the wrong version of JIRA in *pom.xml*. If one particular JIRA URL produces a page with Java reflection errors about a class that changed subtly between versions of JIRA, then you may have compiled your plugin against one version of JIRA and be using it with another incompatible version. The surest sign of this is usually that there are no errors in JIRA log file. Check that the `jira.version` in *pom.xml* matches your local JIRA instance, delete the plugin's *target* directory and rebuild and redeploy the plugin.

Logging

JIRA uses the Apache `log4j` logging framework to record messages in the *log/atlassian-jira.log* file under the `jira.home` directory. This is one easy way to understand what is happening within a plugin during its development. Another way is to use a debugger, as described in "Using a Debugger with JIRA" on page 96.

To use logging within a plugin, first add a `Logger` variable to your source code as shown in Example 1-1. The name of the `Logger`, in this case `com.mycompany.jira.plugins.conditions.MyClass`, can be any unique text but the full Java class name is often a convenient string.

Example 1-1. Example of logging in a plugin

```
package com.mycompany.jira.plugins.conditions;

import org.apache.log4j.Logger;

public class MyClass {

    private static final Logger log = Logger.getLogger(MyClass.class);

    public void MyMethod() {
        log.debug("This message is only seen at the DEBUG log level");
    }

}
```

Next add the following two lines to the file *atlassian-jira/WEB-INF/classes/log4j.properties.* under the JIRA install directory:

```
log4j.logger.com.mycompany.jira.plugins.conditions.MyClass = DEBUG, console, filelog
log4j.additivity.com.mycompany.jira.plugins.conditions.MyClass = false
```

The two lines in *log4j.properties* have a few parameters. The first one is the log level to use (`DEBUG`). The other two (`console` and `filelog`) are the names of *appenders*, which define the places that logging output goes. `filelog` is the appender for *atlassian-jira.log*. The second line with `additivity` stops any parent loggers from logging the same message more than once so you don't see duplicate log entries.

The log level is the level of messages that you want to display. In this case we're using the `DEBUG` log level. A log level of WARN would only show messages created with `log.error()` or `log.warn()`, but not `log.info()` or `log.debug()`.

The most common log levels are in order: `ERROR`, `WARN`, `INFO` and `DEBUG`. If your plugin is using `FATAL` log messages, you're doing something that is at risk of stopping all of JIRA, which seems a bit much for a mere plugin. There is also the less common `TRACE` level which is lower than `DEBUG`.

Restart JIRA to pick up the changes in *log4j.properties* and check the *atlassian-jira.log* file for output lines such as:

```
2010-12-31 15:23:41,123 http-9990-Processor24 DEBUG admin 55421x4x1
129mqbi http://localhost:8800/test.jspa [jira.plugins.conditions.MyClass]
This message is only seen at the DEBUG log level
```

 If you aren't seeing the log messages you expect to see, check the precise spelling of the appropriate entry in *log4j.properties*. Also check that the log level of the message is equal or greater than the current level in *log4j.properties*.

Once the *log4j.properties* file has had the new entries added, they can be temporarily changed at Administration→System→Logging & Profiling. In this case, the next time JIRA is restarted the log level will be set back to the value in *log4j.properties*. Since JIRA 5.0 you can add new entries without restarting JIRA.

Another useful idea is to use the same identifier for all the `log` objects in a plugin across different classes. You can do this by using the same `MyClass.class` identifier in all the classes. Another approach to do the same thing is to declare the `log` variable as `public` in one class and the refer to it as a static variable from the other classes.

The entire `log4j` framework is described in much more detail at *http://logging.apache .org/log4j/1.2/manual.html* and *https://developer.atlassian.com/display/DOCS/Using +your+own+log4j+configuration+for+your+plugin*.

Apache Velocity

Apache Velocity is the templating language used by most JIRA plugins. A templating language allows you to use template files that contain most of the HTML that you want to appear on a web page, and then insert other pieces of HTML dynamically when the template is rendered into HTML by the JIRA server and is returned to a web browser. A plugin's Java source files and its Velocity templates are usually closely related to each other.

Example 1-2 shows a simple example of a Velocity template. If it is stored in a file for a plugin it would usually have a `.vm` suffix and be located somewhere under *src/main/ resources/templates*. Note that Velocity template filenames have to be unique within JIRA, not just within the plugin.

Example 1-2. example.vm—a simple Velocity template

```
## A simple Velocity template file
#if ($value)
    $value.toString()
#else
    This field is empty.
#end
```

Velocity commands and user-defined macros start with a # character. Comments start with ## and Velocity variables begin with a $ character. Velocity files are rendered together with a Velocity context (basically a Java `Map`) that contains the Java objects that each Velocity variable refers to. These objects can be used like any ordinary Java object. For example, Example 1-2 shows the `toString` method being called on the `value` object. The rest of the file is used unchanged in the generated HTML, including any leading spaces and HTML comments.

If you use a variable such as `$myvalue` that is not yet defined, Velocity will display the string $myvalue in the HTML, and may log an error in the JIRA log file. If you'd prefer such an undefined variable to be rendered as an empty string then just use a "quiet reference" to the variable: `$!myvalue`. A quiet reference looks like a Java negation, but they are unrelated.

You can also access a property such as `color` of a variable with `$myvalue.color`. This is the same as using `$myvalue.getColor()` but is more compact.

You will also see references to a variable named `i18n` in many Velocity template files. This is how text messages are internationalized and is described further in "Internationalization" on page 92.

Debugging Velocity template files can be a fiddly task if you're not sure what variables are available for use in the Velocity context. To make this task easier, some of the Velocity contexts used by JIRA add the Velocity context itself as a variable to the context. This let's you display all the variables in the context with Velocity code such as:

```
#foreach($variableName in $ctx.keySet())
    $variableName.toString() - $ctx.get($variableName).getClass().getName()<br/>
#end
```

which will produce a listing of all the variables and their Java classes such as this:

```
ctx - java.util.HashMap
customFieldManager - com.atlassian.jira.issue.managers.DefaultCustomFieldManager
issue - com.atlassian.jira.issue.IssueImpl
field - com.atlassian.jira.issue.fields.CommentSystemField
...
```

In email templates the context is available as `$context`, and for some plugin types it is available as `$ctx`. However, the context is not available for custom field types.

There is some more information about the different Velocity contexts that are used by JIRA at *https://developer.atlassian.com/display/JIRADEV/JIRA+Developer+FAQ*. There is a fairly concise Velocity User Guide available at *http://velocity.apache.org/engine/devel/user-guide.html* and which I recommend reading.

If you are developing Velocity templates that are not delivered in a plugin .jar file, then you can edit *velocity.properties* to have JIRA reload all the .vm files without restarting. This setting and various other changes can also be enabled using the jira.dev.mode flag to JIRA, as described in "JIRA Development Mode" on page 95.

Velocity macros can be defined using the #macro command inline in the same .vm template file, but they can't be shared between the various template files of a plugin.

Including one template file in another can be done with the #parse command. The name of the file to pass to the #parse command is everything below the *src/main/resources* directory, for example:

```
#parse("/templates/com/mycompany/jira/plugins/myplugin/file-to-be-included.vm")
```

The #macro and #parse commands can be combined to make Velocity templates much easier to debug and maintain.

Maven

As introduced in "Creating a JIRA Plugin" on page 2, Apache Maven is a build and deploy tool used by JIRA and many other applications written in Java. This section contains more information about how Maven is used by JIRA plugins.

Maven downloads all the .jar files needed to compile and deploy a plugin using the dependency elements listed in the top-level *pom.xml* file. For example, if a plugin needs to access the HttpServletRequest variable in a method, you will need to add a dependency such as:

```
<dependency>
    <groupId>javax.servlet</groupId>
    <artifactId>servlet-api</artifactId>
    <version>2.5</version>
    <scope>provided</scope>
</dependency>
```

This tells Maven to search the repositories that it has been configured with for a group of releases named "javax.servlet", and then search in those for the file named *servlet-api-2.5.jar*.

The part of dependencies that can be confusing if you're not aware of how it works is the scope element. If there is no scope, then the .jar file is only available during compilation, but the .jar will also be packaged up in the plugin's .jar file. A scope of provided means that the plugin can expect to find it as part of the files shipped with JIRA application, and so the .jar file is *not* added to the plugin .jar file. There are also other scopes such as test that have their own restrictions on when the classes in the .jar file are available.

The Plugin SDK that is used to build JIRA plugins is actually a series of *atlas-* scripts that call a local copy of Maven at *$SDK_HOME/apache-maven/bin/mvn* with a *settings.xml* file that already contains the locations of Atlassian's own Maven repositories. If you're already comfortable with Maven then you can modify your existing Maven installation with those settings and use it to build JIRA plugins instead of the SDK.

More information about Apache Maven can be found at *http://maven.apache.org*. Most Maven behavior is controlled by plugins chosen from the ones listed at *http://maven.apache.org/plugins*. For example, plugin unit tests use the *Surefire* plugin (*http://maven.apache.org/plugins/maven-surefire-plugin*).

Further Reading

Software licensing is a complex matter. One place to start is with the list of different license types shown at *http://www.gnu.org/licenses/license-list.html*. Another helpful resource is the book *Understanding Open Source and Free Software Licensing* by Andrew M. St. Laurent (O'Reilly).

For the specific details of using different IDEs to create JIRA plugins, see *https://developer.atlassian.com/display/DOCS/Generate+Project+Files+for+a+specific+IDE*.

Dan Rosen of Atlassian wrote an excellent four-part blog post about creating Atlassian plugins that starts at *http://blogs.atlassian.com/developer/2011/02/plugin_architecture_episode_iv.This*. html series covers creating a cross-product plugin but contains other useful information as well. The order of the posts is significant: *IV, V, VI* and *I* (think Star Wars).

Another well-written starter tutorial for a JIRA plugin that adds new menus and links is *http://blog.networkedcollaboration.com/2012/02/18/adding-menu-items-to-jira/*.

## CHAPTER 2

Custom Field Types

Overview

This chapter describes how to create your own custom field type using a JIRA plugin. The basics of creating, building and deploying any kind of JIRA plugin were described in "Building and Deploying a Plugin" on page 4. The complete source code for the examples in this and other chapters is available from *https://marketplace.atlassian.com/41293*.

A New Custom Field Type

Each custom field in a JIRA issue has a particular *custom field type*. When a JIRA administrator creates a new custom field the available custom field types are shown, e.g., *Free Text* or *Select List*. To see a new custom field in a JIRA issue, the administrator has to create a custom field of the chosen type and also make sure that it is associated with the desired projects, issue types and screens.

Our example is a new custom field type for currency values. This type of custom field is something for which there are several long-standing feature requests at Atlassian, e.g., *JRA-3873*. We'll start off with just one currency, whatever the local one is for the Java JVM used by JIRA. Then we'll add more features after that.

The first thing to consider is whether we can build on an existing JIRA custom field type. These standard types are defined in the JIRA file *system-customfieldtypes-plugin.xml*. Since the data we want to store is a number, the best class to extend for this example is the `com.atlassian.jira.issue.customfields.impl.NumberCFType` class, which is what is used by the standard *Number Field* custom field type in JIRA.

For our first effort, we want to create and edit the value in the custom field, display the correct currency symbol and use the correct number of decimal places and separator for thousands. For example, the number `2000.123` should be displayed as "$2,000.12" in the USA and as "2 000,12€" in France.

Creating the plugin for the new custom field type will involve the following steps, as described in "Creating a JIRA Plugin" on page 2:

1. Generate an empty JIRA plugin using the Atlassian Plugin SDK.

2. Define how the plugin will use the Java and Velocity files with the *atlassian-plugin.xml* file.

3. Create the Java source code to define how the custom field type behaves. This is the class that implements the standard JIRA `CustomFieldType` interface. This interface is discussed in more detail in "CustomFieldType Methods" on page 39.

4. Add some Velocity template files to control how the field appears when viewing and editing an issue.

Generating an Empty Plugin

Download the Atlassian Plugin SDK from *https://developer.atlassian.com/display/DOCS/Set+up+the+Atlassian+Plugin+SDK+and+Build+a+Project* and unpack it locally. Think of a unique and brief name for your plugin. In this case we're going to use "currency". To generate the plugin from a Unix or OSX command line prompt interactively, run:

```
$SDK_HOME/bin/atlas-create-jira-plugin
```

Windows works as well with the usual changes. Then answer the prompts as follows:

```
Define value for groupId: : com.mycompany.jira.plugins
Define value for artifactId: : currency
Define value for version: 1.0-SNAPSHOT: : 5.1.0
Define value for package: com.mycompany.jira.plugins: :
        com.mycompany.jira.plugins.currency
```

The `artifactId` and `groupId` values appear in the generated Maven *pom.xml* file. They're also used in the *atlassian-plugin.xml* file to create a unique key for your plugin: `com.mycompany.jira.plugins.currency`. The `version` is used in *pom.xml* and will be part of the name of the plugin's deployable .jar file later on. The `package` argument controls the name of the Java package that your source code will use.

 It's a good idea to add all the generated files in the *currency* directory to version control before you start modifying them. You can leave the generated *currency/src/test* directory in place even if you haven't written any tests.

Edit the generated *pom.xml* file to set the organization details and a description of the plugin. The precise details of what is allowed in a *pom.xml* file can be found at *http://maven.apache.org/pom.html#More_Project_Information*.

Check that the new skeleton plugin at least compiles with the *atlas-package* command. This should download a number of other dependencies, then compile everything and package it up into a .jar file named *target/currency-5.1.0.jar*.

The *atlas-run* command will start up a local instance of JIRA at `http://localhost:2990/jira` and deploy the plugin there. The user name and password is **admin** and **admin**. You can also deploy the plugin .jar file as you would any other JIRA plugin by copying it to *jira.home/data/plugins/installed-plugins* as noted in the section "Building and Deploying a Plugin" on page 4.

 As of JIRA 4.3, custom field type plugins cannot be redeployed with the *atlas-cli, pi* commands. JIRA has to be restarted after a new version of a custom field type plugin is installed or updated. Later versions of JIRA should allow custom fields to be updated without restarting JIRA.

Adding a customfield-type to atlassian-plugin.xml

The next step is to add a `customfield-type` element to *src/main/resources/atlassian-plugin.xml*. This file and the `customfield-type` element are shown in Example 2-1.

Example 2-1. The atlassian-plugin.xml file for the currency custom field type

```
<atlassian-plugin key="${project.groupId}.${project.artifactId}" ❶
                  name="${project.name}"
                  plugins-version="2"> ❷
    <plugin-info> ❸
        <description>${project.description}</description>
        <version>${project.version}</version>
        <vendor name="${project.organization.name}"
                url="${project.organization.url}" />
    </plugin-info>

    <customfield-type key="currency-field" ❹
                      name="Currency" ❺
                      class="com.mycompany.jira.plugins.currency.CurrencyCFType"> ❻
        <description>
          A custom field type for a currency.
        </description>

        <resource type="velocity"
                  name="view"
              location="templates/com/mycompany/jira/plugins/currency/view.vm"/> ❼
        <resource type="velocity"
                  name="edit"
              location="templates/com/mycompany/jira/plugins/currency/edit.vm"/> ❽
    </customfield-type>

</atlassian-plugin>
```

❶ The unique key for the plugin uses the variables from *pom.xml* which were defined when the plugin was created. This is a string (com.mycompany.jira.plugins. currency), not a Java package name, even though they appear identical.

❷ This is a version two plugin; see the section "Version One, Version Two and Version Three Plugins" on page 95.

❸ This element is automatically generated by the SDK and you shouldn't need to change it.

❹ The identifier for the new custom field type, unique within *atlassian-plugin.xml*. If this is changed later on, JIRA may have custom fields that it doesn't know what to do with, so it just hides them.

❺ The name of the custom field type as it appears in JIRA. This can be changed at any time.

❻ The Java class that implements the custom field type.

❼ The Velocity template file used to view the field's value.

❽ The Velocity template file used to edit the field's value or create a new value.

Newer versions of the SDK have a *atlas-create-jira-plugin-module* command which will prompt you for what kind of plugin module you want to add to an existing *atlassian-plugin.xml* file. This command can help save some typing.

If you have more than one custom field type, then you would have a customfield-type element for each one. It's perfectly fine for different custom field types to use the same Java class or Velocity templates in different combinations.

JIRA plugins can be internationalized so they can use other languages. This is omitted from all the samples shown in this book for brevity, but is instead covered in the section "Internationalization" on page 92.

Creating the CustomFieldType Class

Now we need to create the class that implements the CustomFieldType interface and actually provides the functionality for the new custom field type. It's a common convention to add the suffix "CFType" for "Custom Field Type" to the name of this class. In the class attribute of the customfield-type element we have used the name CurrencyCFType.

Create a new file named src/main/java/com/mycompany/jira/plugins/currency/ CurrencyCFType.java containing the source shown in Example 2-2, and add it to version control.

Example 2-2. CurrencyCFType.java

```
package com.mycompany.jira.plugins.currency;
```

```
import com.atlassian.jira.issue.customfields.converters.DoubleConverter;
import com.atlassian.jira.issue.customfields.impl.NumberCFType;
import com.atlassian.jira.issue.customfields.manager.GenericConfigManager;
import com.atlassian.jira.issue.customfields.persistence.CustomFieldValuePersister;

/**
 * A custom field type that displays numbers as the local currency.
 * The transport object is a Double, just like the parent class.
 */
public class CurrencyCFType extends NumberCFType {


    public CurrencyCFType(final CustomFieldValuePersister customFieldValuePersister,
                          final DoubleConverter doubleConverter,
                          final GenericConfigManager genericConfigManager) {
        super(customFieldValuePersister,
              doubleConverter,
              genericConfigManager);
    }


}
```

Example 2-2 doesn't do anything different from its NumberCFType parent class, but compiling and deploying it at this stage of development helps to catch any problems with how the constructor's arguments are injected (see the section "Troubleshooting a Build" on page 9).

The *transport object* for a custom field type mentioned in the comment in Example 2-2 is defined as the type of the Java Object used within JIRA to represent a field's value in a given issue. For the CurrencyCFType class the transport object is a Double. A more complex custom field type, as described in "Fields with Multiple Values" on page 38, can have a transport object that is a Collection of the *singular object* type, which is itself another Java Object. For now we'll just use a Double transport object for simplicity.

Next we can start to modify the *CurrencyCFType.java* file to make the example do what we want. In Example 2-3, we have added a new method getVelocityParameters that overrides the method of the same name in the parent class. This method returns a Map that will contain the extra variables used to render the Velocity template files defined in "Adding Velocity Template Files" on page 22. In this case we've added a variable currencySymbol that contains the symbol for the local currency. We are using the standard Java java.util.Currency class for this information.

Example 2-3. Updated CurrencyCFType.java

```
package com.mycompany.jira.plugins.currency;

import com.atlassian.jira.issue.customfields.converters.DoubleConverter;
import com.atlassian.jira.issue.customfields.impl.NumberCFType;
import com.atlassian.jira.issue.customfields.manager.GenericConfigManager;
import com.atlassian.jira.issue.customfields.persistence.CustomFieldValuePersister;
import com.atlassian.jira.issue.Issue;
```

```
import com.atlassian.jira.issue.fields.CustomField;
import com.atlassian.jira.issue.fields.layout.field.FieldLayoutItem;
import java.util.Currency;
import java.util.Map;
import java.util.HashMap;

public class CurrencyCFType extends NumberCFType {

    public CurrencyCFType(final CustomFieldValuePersister customFieldValuePersister,
                          final DoubleConverter doubleConverter,
                          final GenericConfigManager genericConfigManager) {
        super(customFieldValuePersister,
              doubleConverter,
              genericConfigManager);
    }

    public Map<String, Object> getVelocityParameters(final Issue issue,
                                                     final CustomField field,
                                                     final FieldLayoutItem
                                                         fieldLayoutItem) {
        final Map<String, Object> map = super.getVelocityParameters(issue, field,
                                                         fieldLayoutItem);
        String symbol = Currency.getInstance(getI18nBean().getLocale()).getSymbol();
        map.put("currencySymbol", symbol);
        log.debug("Currency symbol is " + symbol);
        return map;
    }

}
```

Another variable that is already present in the Velocity parameters `Map` is `numberTool`, which is an instance of the JIRA `NumberTool` class. The `NumberTool` class is a general purpose class for displaying numbers in different formats and will be used in the *view.vm* Velocity template file later on.

The `numberTool` variable was added in the same `getVelocityParameters` method but in the parent `NumberCFType` class. It's important to call the `super.getVelocityParameters` method so that variables such as `numberTool` that were added by the parent class are not dropped.

The `log` variable is inherited from a parent class `AbstractSingleFieldType` and is used by all custom field types. Since it's not used very frequently, we can safely reuse it for our examples. The changes to the *log4j.properties* file to do this are shown in the section "Troubleshooting the Plugin" on page 25.

Adding Velocity Template Files

Next we add the Velocity template files for the example. As described in "Apache Velocity" on page 12, Velocity is the template language used by JIRA to generate HTML pages. Whatever you add to a template file will appear in the web page for a custom field as part of an issue. There are two main Velocity resources used by a custom field type: *view* and *edit*. The actual filenames used for each of these are defined in *atlassian-plugin.xml* as `resource` elements.

 The filenames used for Velocity templates have to be unique across all plugins installed in JIRA, so it's common to see the same directory structure under the *templates* directory as used in the Java source directory. You can use any unique name you want though.

The original *Number Field* custom field type has a view resource with a template file named *view-number.vm* that simply contains:

```
#if ($value)
    $!numberTool.format($value)
#end
```

We can copy this text directly into a new file *templates/com/mycompany/jira/plugins/currency/view.vm* and modify it as shown in Example 2-4.

Example 2-4. view.vm Velocity template file for currency

```
## The string 'currency' makes format() treat the value as a currency
#if ($value)
    $!numberTool.format('currency', $value)
#end
```

The `NumberTool` class mentioned in the section "Creating the CustomFieldType Class" on page 20 has a convenient instance of the same `format` method that will display a number as a local currency, as circled in Figure 2-1. In this case, the local currency symbol is $ for the US dollar.

Details	
Type:	🐞 Bug
Priority:	⬆ Major
Affects Version/s:	None
Component/s:	None
Labels:	None ✎
Amount:	($19.95)

Figure 2-1. Viewing a Currency custom field

The second and final template file that we need to create is *templates/com/mycompany/jira/plugins/currency/edit.vm*. Once again the contents shown in Example 2-5 are very similar to the *edit-number.vm* template file used by the parent class `NumberCFType` in *system-customfieldtypes-plugin.xml*.

Example 2-5. edit.vm Velocity template file

```
#customControlHeader ($action $customField.id \  ❶
    $customField.name $fieldLayoutItem.required $displayParameters $auiparams )
$currencySymbol  ❷
<input style="width:200px"
       id="$customField.id"
       name="$customField.id"  ❸
       type="text"
       value="$textutils.htmlEncode($!value)" />  ❹
#customControlFooter ($action $customField.id \
    $fieldLayoutItem.fieldDescription $displayParameters $auiparams )
```

❶ This provides the standard header and footer HTML for custom fields. Velocity macros such as *customControlHeader* and *customControlFooter* appear on a single line in the source code for this chapter.

❷ This is the variable we added to the Velocity context in `getVelocityParameters` in Example 2-3.

❸ This is the unique identifier for this custom field instance and is a string such as `customfield_10010`.

❹ This is the current value of the custom field in the issue. The $! is a quiet reference so that if there is no current value, then an empty string is shown.

The main change from the original edit template is the addition of the currency symbol with `$currencySymbol`. The original `class` attribute was also replaced with `style="width:200px"` to set the width of the HTML input field. The resulting HTML for editing the custom field is shown in Figure 2-2 with the `$currencySymbol` circled. Our first example is working now.

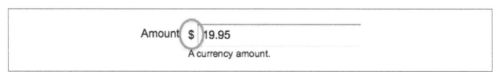

Figure 2-2. Editing a Currency custom field also shows the local currency symbol

As an aside, there are a few other Velocity resources that you may come across in custom field type plugins. The `column-view` resource controls how a field's value appears in the Issue Navigator. If this is not set then it is just the same as the `view` resource. The `xml` resource defines how the field appears in an XML view of an issue in the Issue Navigator. Note that an XML backup of JIRA is a representation of the database contents as is different from what is seen in an issue. Less commonly-used resources are `edit-default` for what a default value looks like when you're setting it and `bulk-move` for when more than one issue is being updated.

Troubleshooting the Plugin

Once you've deployed the new plugin, you should be able to add a new custom field to JIRA and see the new field type offered as a choice. If it doesn't appear, check that the plugin is present and that the custom field type module is correctly enabled at Administration→Plugins.

If the plugin doesn't appear as a choice, it may well be due to an error in the *atlassian-plugin.xml* file. Check the JIRA log file for error messages such as "Cannot parse XML plugin descriptor", noting that the actual line that a syntax error appears on is usually logged in a second error message after the first one.

We didn't define a searcher for the new custom field type, so the new custom field won't appear in the list of fields to search on in the Issue Navigator. Chapter 4 discusses how to add searchers to custom field types.

If a custom field type plugin has errors and isn't loaded, then all the custom fields of that type won't appear in any issues or in the list of custom fields at Administration→Custom Fields. However, the underlying data for that field is still present in the database and the fields will reappear when the plugin is successfully loaded. This also means that data from old custom fields is never discarded from JIRA's database; it just stops being used.

As described in "Logging" on page 11, a plugin can emit log messages to the JIRA log file. This can be very helpful during plugin development. There is a Logger defined in a higher parent class AbstractSingleFieldType that can be used with the following lines in *log4j.properties*.

```
log4j.logger.com.atlassian.jira.issue.customfields.impl.
    AbstractSingleFieldType = DEBUG, console, filelog
log4j.additivity.com.atlassian.jira.issue.customfields.impl.
    AbstractSingleFieldType = false
```

Many developers prefer to define a single logger for all the messages from a plugin. See "Logging" on page 11 for details on how to do that.

It's worth checking again that the template files that you created are actually the ones being used. Template files names must be unique across all of JIRA and all JIRA plugins. So naming a template something like "view.vm" is only safe if you use a unique directory name. Otherwise it should be named something like "currency-view.vm".

Extending the Plugin

Let's add some more functionality to the plugin. This will also demonstrate how the data in the custom field is handled. We'll now allow a user to append "K" or "M" when editing the value in the custom field. The value will then be multiplied by a thousand or a million respectively. This doesn't change the type of what is being stored in the field; it's simply syntactic sugar to avoid typing lots of zeroes when editing a value.

Example 2-6 shows how the `getSingularObjectFromString` method in `CurrencyCFType` can be overridden to modify the value in the field.

Example 2-6. Adding the M and K Suffixes to CurrencyCFType.java

```java
import com.atlassian.jira.issue.customfields.impl.FieldValidationException;

    /**
     * Handle the optional M and K suffixes.
     *
     * Note that in JIRA 4.x this method returned an Object.
     */
    public Double getSingularObjectFromString(String numberString)
        throws FieldValidationException {
        log.debug("getSingularObjectFromString: " + numberString);

        double multiplier = 1.0;
        if (numberString.endsWith("K") || numberString.endsWith("k")) {
            multiplier = 1000.0;
        }
        if (numberString.endsWith("M") || numberString.endsWith("m")) {
            multiplier = 1000000.0;
        }

        // Remove the multiplier character
        if (multiplier > 1.0) {
            numberString = numberString.substring(0, numberString.length() - 1);
        }

        // Use the parent's method to get the actual value of the field
        // Prior to JIRA 5.0 this needed a cast
        Double value = super.getSingularObjectFromString(numberString);
        // Adjust the value appropriately
        value = value * multiplier;

        // Copied from DoubleConverterImpl where this is private
        Double MAX_VALUE = new Double("100000000000000"); // 14 zeroes
        if (value.compareTo(MAX_VALUE) > 0) {
            throw new FieldValidationException("The value " +
 numberString + " is larger than the maximum value allowed:  " + MAX_VALUE);
        }

        return value;
    }
```

The `getSingularObjectFromString` method is called multiple times from various methods of `CustomFieldType` so expect to see multiple log messages about it. The invocation that matters in this case is the one from `getValueFromCustomFieldParams` in the parent class `AbstractSingleFieldType`. That method is what JIRA uses to convert the string returned after editing a field into a value used by the field within JIRA.

Summary

This chapter showed how to create a new custom field type to display a number as an amount in the local currency. It also showed how the value entered by a user in an edit screen can be modified. The next chapter describes even farther-reaching changes to the currency example.

Further Reading

An Atlassian tutorial about creating a new JIRA 5.0 custom field type can now be found at *https://developer.atlassian.com/display/JIRADEV/Plugin+Tutorial+-+Creating+a +Custom+Field+in+JIRA*. It creates a custom field type for storing dollar amounts with two decimal places.

For more information about what changed in JIRA 5.0 with custom fields see *https:// developer.atlassian.com/display/JIRADEV/Java+API+Changes+in+JIRA+5.0#JavaA PIChangesinJIRA50-CustomFieldTypes*. There were some major changes in the class hierarchy, and most classes now have a Java generic as a parameter instead of just using an Object as before.

## CHAPTER 3

Advanced Custom Field Types

Overview

This chapter describes some more advanced aspects of custom field plugins, including configuration and fields that contain multiple values. The first example in this chapter builds on the simpler example introduced in Chapter 2. The source code for all the examples in this chapter is available at *https://marketplace.atlassian.com/41293*.

Adding Configuration to a Custom Field

Different types of custom fields are configured differently. For example, many custom fields can have a default value configured. *Select List* custom fields can have their options (choices) configured. This section shows how to configure the *Currency* custom field type of Chapter 2 to display its value in a specific currency such as Euro (€) or Pound (£). The actual value stored in the field is unchanged, but what is seen in the field in an issue should change according to the chosen type of currency.

JIRA also allows different *contexts* to be configured for each custom field. This is how you can have different sets of options for a *Select List* in different projects and issue types. The custom field configuration described here also supports choosing different currencies for different custom field contexts.

 JIRA also allows you to have many custom fields all with the same type and same name, since it uses a unique custom field id internally for each field. However this is usually too confusing in practice, so I don't recommend it. Use contexts instead.

The first thing to do is to decide what is going to be stored about the configuration for a field. In this case we will store the unique name of a Java `Locale` which will determine which currency will be used. The `Locale` class is the standard Java class for customizations for different languages and countries.

To configure a currency we will need to define a new class that implements the interface com.atlassian.jira.issue.fields.config.FieldConfigItemType. This is the same interface that is implemented by the classes that provide a default configuration or options configuration for a custom field.

We'll also need to define a new web page in JIRA to let us choose from a list of currencies and then save our choice. To save the chosen configuration, we're going to use the propertyentry database table described in the section "Storing Data with Property-Set" on page 77.

There are several ways to add new pages to JIRA for things like configuring a plugin. One approach that uses a servlet plugin module type is becoming more common with newer versions of JIRA. This approach is described in the tutorial at *https://developer .atlassian.com/display/DOCS/Plugin+tutorial+-+Writing+an+Admin+Configuration +Screen*.

A New FieldConfigItemType

All configuration items in JIRA implement the FieldConfigItemType interface. These classes are sometimes referred to as "ConfigItem" classes. Example 3-1 shows the new CurrencyConfigItem class for this example.

Example 3-1. CurrencyConfigItem.java

```
package com.mycompany.jira.plugins.currency;

import com.atlassian.jira.issue.Issue;
import com.atlassian.jira.issue.fields.config.FieldConfig;
import com.atlassian.jira.issue.fields.config.FieldConfigItemType;
import com.atlassian.jira.issue.fields.layout.field.FieldLayoutItem;
import java.util.Currency;
import java.util.Locale;
import java.util.HashMap;
import java.util.Map;

public class CurrencyConfigItem implements FieldConfigItemType {

    // The name of this kind of configuration, as seen in the field
    // configuration scheme
    public String getDisplayName() {
        return "Currency";
    }

    // This is the text shown in the field configuration screen
    public String getDisplayNameKey() {
        return "Selected Currency";
    }

    // This is the current value as shown in the field configuration screen
    public String getViewHtml(FieldConfig fieldConfig,
                              FieldLayoutItem fieldLayoutItem) {
```

```
        Locale locale = DAO.getCurrentLocale(fieldConfig);
        return DAO.getDisplayValue(locale);
    }



    // The unique identifier for this kind of configuration, and also the
    // key for the $configs Map used in edit.vm
    public String getObjectKey() {
        return "currencyconfig";
    }

    // Return the Object used in the Velocity edit context in $configs
    public Object getConfigurationObject(Issue issue, FieldConfig config) {
        Map result - new HashMap();
        result.put("currencyLocale", DAO.getCurrentLocale(config));
        result.put("currencySymbol", DAO.getCurrentSymbol(config));
        return result;
    }

    // Where the Edit link should redirect to when it's clicked on
    public String getBaseEditUrl() {
        return "EditCurrencyConfig.jspa";
    }

}
```

The `FieldConfig` variable that is passed into several of the methods in `Currency ConfigItem` is what represents the context of a custom field. The `DAO` (Data Access Object) class is responsible for storing the configuration data in the database and is described further in "Configuration Storage" on page 38.

The field configuration screen in Figure 3-1 shows what configuring the new `Config Item` looks like in JIRA. The string "Selected Currency" from the `getDisplayNameKey` method can be seen, as can two contexts with a different currency in each context.

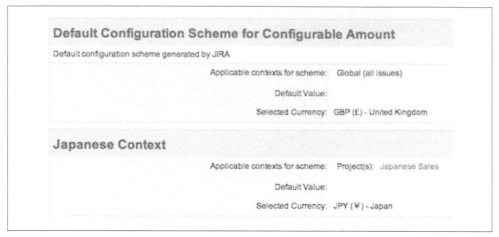

Figure 3-1. Configuring a Currency Custom Field

Once the new `CurrencyConfigItem` class exists, we can refer to it in the main `Currency CFType` class. The method to override to do this is `getConfigurationItemTypes`, as shown in Example 3-2. Make sure to only add to the existing list of ConfigItems, not replace it, or you won't be able to set a default value for the new custom field type.

Example 3-2. Adding the CurrencyConfigItem to CurrencyCFType.java

```
public List<FieldConfigItemType> getConfigurationItemTypes() {
    final List<FieldConfigItemType> configurationItemTypes =
        super.getConfigurationItemTypes();
    configurationItemTypes.add(new CurrencyConfigItem());
    return configurationItemTypes;
}

public Map<String, Object> getVelocityParameters(final Issue issue,
                                                 final CustomField field,
                                                 final FieldLayoutItem
                                                         fieldLayoutItem) {
    final Map<String, Object> map = super.getVelocityParameters(issue, field,
                                                 fieldLayoutItem);

    // This method is also called to get the default value, in
    // which case issue is null so we can't use it to add currencyLocale
    if (issue == null) {
        return map;
    }

    FieldConfig fieldConfig = field.getRelevantConfig(issue);
    // Get the stored configuration choice
    map.put("currencyLocale", DAO.getCurrentLocale(fieldConfig));

    return map;
}
```

We also need to make a small change in Example 3-2 to the `getVelocityParameters` method to add the `currencyLocale` variable. This variable will contain the `Locale` object for the chosen currency so that the *view.vm* Velocity template file shown in Example 3-3 can use it to display the value for the field correctly.

Example 3-3. view.vm Velocity template file

```
#if ($value)
    #if ($currencyLocale)
      $!numberTool.format('currency', $value, $currencyLocale)
    #else
      ## This is true when displaying the current default value
      $!numberTool.format($value)
    #end
#end
```

 The `DefaultValueConfigItem` class (not shown here) is what is used for configuring default values. The way that class works means that there is no issue or context that we can use to decide which currency symbol to use—so we just display the raw number when we need to show the default value.

The updated *edit.vm* Velocity template that we use to edit the value in the field itself (not the configuration) is shown in Example 3-4. The only change from Example 2-5 is that we are now accessing the `currencySymbol` variable via the `$configs` variable using the string defined in the `getObjectKey` method in *CurrencyConfigItem.java*. The Velocity macros such as *customControlHeader* appear on a single line in the source code for this chapter.

Example 3-4. edit.vm Velocity template file

```
#customControlHeader ($action $customField.id \
    $customField.name $fieldLayoutItem.required $displayParameters $auiparams )
#set($configObj = $configs.get("currencyconfig")) ❶
#set ($currencySymbol = $configObj.get("currencySymbol")) ❷
$currencySymbol
<input style="width:200px"
       id="$customField.id"
       name="$customField.id"
       type="text"
       value="$textutils.htmlEncode($!value)" />
#customControlFooter ($action $customField.id \
    $fieldLayoutItem.fieldDescription $displayParameters $auiparams )
```

❶ `currencyconfig` is the `String` returned by the `getObjectKey` method in Example 3-1.

❷ `currencySymbol` was added to the `Map` returned by the `getConfigurationObject` method in Example 3-1.

Velocity Templates and a WebWork Action

So far we've defined a new type of configuration and updated the CurrencyCFType class and Velocity template files to supply the new information. We also need a new web page to allow us to choose a particular currency.

The way that JIRA defines web pages is with the *WebWork* web application framework (see "WebWork" on page 45 for more information). The core mapping from the standard JIRA URLs to their Java classes and the templates that generate the HTML for each web page is in a file named *actions.xml*. We can define new web pages in plugins in a similar way by using the webwork plugin module type.

Example 3-5 shows how this webwork element can be used in the *atlassian-plugin.xml* file. Each action element defines a new "alias" and the class it uses. The alias plus ".jspa" is the URL for the new web page.

Example 3-5. The webwork element in atlassian-plugin.xml

```
<webwork1 key="currencyconfigaction"
          name="Currency configuration action"
          class="java.lang.Object">
  <description>
    The action for editing a currency custom field type configuration.
  </description>

  <actions>
    <action name="com.mycompany.jira.plugins.currency.EditConfiguration" ❶
            alias="EditCurrencyConfig"> ❷
      <view name="input">
        /templates/com/mycompany/jira/plugins/currency/edit-config.vm
      </view> ❸
    </action>
  </actions> ❹
</webwork1>
```

❶ The action class EditConfiguration is what is called when an administrator browses to http://jira.example.com/secure/admin/EditCurrencyConfig.jspa.

❷ This is what the EditCurrencyConfig.jspa string returned from the getBaseEditUrl method in Example 3-1 referred to.

❸ The view element controls which Velocity template will be rendered to display the new page. In this case we only have a single template but there are often more.

❹ There is no error if you accidentally put an action element outside the actions element.

Now that we've associated a new URL with a Velocity template and an Action class, let's look at the new template. The HTML that offers a select list of currency choices and submits one in a form when a button is clicked is pretty ordinary, as shown in Example 3-6. In this case the same HTML is used for both viewing and editing the configuration. The resulting web page is shown in Figure 3-2.

Figure 3-2. Choosing a Currency for a field named Amount (Configurable)

Example 3-6. edit-config.vm Velocity template file

```
<html>
  <head>
    <title>$i18n.getText('common.words.configure')
        $action.getCustomField().getName()</title> ❶
    <meta content="admin" name="decorator" /> ❷
    <link rel="stylesheet" type="text/css" media="print"
      href="/styles/combined-printable.css">
      <link type="text/css" rel="StyleSheet" media="all" href="/styles/combined.css"/>
  </head>
  <body>

<h2 class="formtitle">
  $i18n.getText('common.words.configure') $action.getCustomField().getName()
</h2>
<p>
  Select a currency for displaying the value of the currency field.
</p>

<form action="EditCurrencyConfig.jspa" method="post"> ❸

  <table>
    <tr>
      <td>
        Currency:
      </td>

      <td>
        <select id="localestr" name="localestr"> ❹
          #set ($currencyOptions = $action.getCurrencies()) ❺
          #foreach ($currencyOption in $currencyOptions)
            #set ($localeId = $currencyOption.getId())
            <option value="$localeId"
                    #if ($action.isSelected($localeId)) selected #end ❻
                    >
              $currencyOption.getDisplayValue()
            </option>
          #end
        </select>
      </td>

    <td>
    <input type="submit"
              name="Save"
              id="Save"
              value="$i18n.getText('common.words.done')"
```

```
            accesskey="S"
            title="Press Ctrl+S to submit form"
            class="spaced"
            />
    </td>
  </tr>
</table>

<input type="hidden" name="fieldConfigId" value="$fieldConfigId"> ❼

</form>

  </body>
</html>
```

❶ The $action variable is the WebWork Action class EditConfiguration shown in Example 3-7. The $i18n variable is for internationalization of text.

❷ Without the admin decorator, none of the other JIRA menu items appear.

❸ The form element's action attribute is the alias of the web page, plus ".jspa". Use a post method for a regular HTML form.

❹ The name "localestr" must be matched by a public method setLocalestr in the action's class (using *JavaBean* naming conventions). The value passed in localestr is a unique identifier for each locale, which is later used to select the appropriate currency.

❺ getCurrencies returns a List of CurrencyOption objects that contain an id that will become localestr, and a display value for the select list.

❻ Calls the isSelected method in EditConfiguration to check if this option is the currently chosen one.

❼ The fieldConfigId defines the context for this configuration and is used by the parent class AbstractEditConfigurationItemAction.

Finally let's see the Action class that the new configuration web page uses. Example 3-1 shows the main methods of *EditConfiguration.java*.

When the URL is first visited, doValidate is called and then if that passes, the do Execute method is called to decide which view resource to use. The localestr variable won't be set until the HTML form is submitted with a value in the select field.

Example 3-7. EditConfiguration.java

```
public class EditConfiguration extends AbstractEditConfigurationItemAction {

    // The chosen locale (as a string) and its currency. The format is
    // Language[_Country[_Variant]]. For example, en_US
    private String localestr;

    // This method is set when the HTML form is submitted because
    // the name of the HTML input element is "localestr"
```

```java
    public void setLocalestr(String value) {
        this.localestr = value;
    }

    public String getLocalestr() {
        return this.localestr;
    }

    // When the form is submitted, check the value before doing anything else
    protected void doValidation() {
        String lstr = getLocalestr();
        log.debug("Entering doValidation with " + lstr);
        if (lstr == null) {
            // Nothing to check yet until a choice is submitted
            return;
        }
        String[] parts = lstr.split("_");
        if (parts.length < 1 || parts.length > 3) {
            addErrorMessage("Unable to parse the Locale string: " +
                            lstr + " has " + parts.length + " parts");
        }
    }

    // Process the submitted form and its chosen currency
    protected String doExecute() throws Exception {
        if (!isHasPermission(Permissions.ADMINISTER)) {
            return "securitybreach";
        }

        // The first time the page is loaded retrieve any existing configuration
        if (getLocalestr() == null) {
            setLocalestr(DAO.retrieveStoredValue(getFieldConfig()));
        }

        // Save the configured currency choice
        DAO.updateStoredValue(getFieldConfig(), getLocalestr());

        // Redirect to the custom field configuration screen
        String save = request.getParameter("Save");
        if (save != null && save.equals("Save")) {
            setReturnUrl("/secure/admin/ConfigureCustomField!default.jspa?customFieldId="
            + getFieldConfig().getCustomField().getIdAsLong().toString());
            return getRedirect("not used");
        }

        // This is the name of the Velocity view resource in the action element
        return "input";
    }

    // Other methods omitted for brevity
}
```

The **request** variable used in **doExecute** is the underlying HttpServletRequest object that was received by JIRA from the browser. Accessing it requires adding a dependency to the plugin's *pom.xml* file:

```
<dependency>
    <groupId>javax.servlet</groupId>
    <artifactId>servlet-api</artifactId>
    <version>2.5</version>
    <scope>provided</scope>
</dependency>
```

Configuration Storage

Once a locale and its associated currency have been chosen, we need to save that choice somewhere. The `DAO` (Data Access Object) class does that for this plugin. It uses the `propertyentry` database table as described in the section "Storing Data with Property-Set" on page 77.

The two main methods in *DAO.java* are `retrieveStoredValue` and `updateStoredValue`. Both of these methods work with a String value, and both require a `FieldConfig` parameter, which specifies the context for a custom field.

This class also contains some convenience methods for converting the stored value to a `Locale` object, and for finding the currency symbol for a given `Locale`. The case where no value has been defined yet is handled by the `doExecute` method in `EditConfigura` `tion` in Example 3-7, not at the storage level.

Configuration Summary

The modified `currency` custom field type now displays the chosen currency symbol and the correctly formatted value. For example, Figure 3-3 shows a currency field that has been configured to use a French locale which uses the € currency symbol, spaces for the thousands separator and a comma for the decimal point.

Figure 3-3. A Configured Currency Field

Fields with Multiple Values

The next example shows a custom field that contains multiple values. One example of such a field is the standard *Multi Select* custom field type which allows you to choose multiple options.

As introduced in "Creating the CustomFieldType Class" on page 20, the transport object is the Java class that represents the field's value inside JIRA. A transport object can be a class such as a `String` or a `Collection` of *singular objects*. The class for the singular object can also be any Java class. For this example we'll create a new class named `Carrier` for the singular object. The `Carrier` class has two fields—a numeric amount field and a note field, which is some text about the amount field:

```
private Double amount;    // e.g., 42.0
private String note;      // e.g., The answer
```

The first thing to do is to decide how the data in a `Carrier` object will be stored in the database. A simple way to do this is to use the `TYPE_UNLIMITED_TEXT` database type and to convert each `Carrier` object into a string such as "42.0###The answer". We'll use the separator ###, since it is unlikely to occur in the note variable itself. We'll also remove it from any given value for note just to be safe.

The next few sections also cover some of the details about the `CustomFieldType` interface and other interfaces that custom field types commonly implement.

CustomFieldType Methods

The example's custom field type class will implement the `CustomFieldType` interface as usual, but instead will extend a class higher up in the inheritance hierarchy than `NumberCFType`. The class we will extend is `AbstractCustomFieldType` and it's at the root of most classes that implement `CustomFieldType`.

> The methods in the `CustomFieldType` interface with "SingularObject" in their name refer to the singular object, in this example a `Carrier` object. All other methods in JIRA 4 custom fields that refer to an `Object` are referring the transport object, e.g., a `Collection` of `Carrier` objects. JIRA 5 removed the use of Object in most custom field methods.
>
> For more information about what changed in JIRA 5.0 with custom fields see *https://developer.atlassian.com/display/JIRADEV/Java+API +Changes+in+JIRA+5.0#JavaAPIChangesinJIRA50-CustomField Types*. There were some major changes in the class hierarchy, and most classes now have a Java generic as a parameter instead of just using an `Object` as before.

There are two objects that are typically injected into the constructor of a custom field type's class. The first is a `CustomFieldValuePersister` persister object, which is what will actually interact with the database. The second is a `GenericConfigManager` object that is used for storing and retrieving default values for the custom field. Other objects are injected into the constructor as needed—for example, the `DoubleConverter` in Example 2-2.

The first set of methods to consider are the ones that the custom field type uses to interact with the database in some way.

`getSingularObjectFromString()`
>   This method converts a string taken from the database such as "42.0###The answer" into a `Carrier` object. A null value means that there is no such object defined.

`Collection<Carrier> getValueFromIssue(CustomField field, Issue issue)`

> This is the main method for extracting what a field contains for a given issue. It uses the persister to retrieve the values from the database for the issue, converts each value into a `Carrier` object and then puts all the `Carrier` objects into a transport object `Collection`. A null value means that this field has no value stored for the given issue. This is one of the methods that used to return an `Object` before JIRA 5.0

`createValue(CustomField field, Issue issue, Collection<Carrier> value)`
`updateValue(CustomField field, Issue issue, Collection<Carrier> value)`

> These methods create a new value or update an existing value for the field in the given issue. The persister that does this expects a `Collection` of `Strings` to store, so both of these methods call the method `getDbValueFromCollection` to help with that.

`getDbValueFromCollection()`

> A private convenience method found in many custom field type classes, sometimes with a different name. It is used to convert a transport object (e.g., a `Collection` of `Carrier` objects) to a `Collection` of `Strings` for storing in the database.

`setDefaultValue(FieldConfig fieldConfig, Collection<Carrier> value)`

> Convert a transport object (a `Collection` of `Carrier` objects) to its database representation and store it in the database in the genericconfiguration table.

`Collection<Carrier> getDefaultValue(FieldConfig fieldConfig)`

> Retrieve a default value, if any, from the database and convert it to a transport object (a `Collection` of `Carrier` objects). The `FieldConfig` object is what represents the context of each default value in a custom field.

The next set of methods to consider are the ones that interact with a web page in some way. All values from web pages arrive at a custom field type object as part of a `Custom FieldParams` object, which is a holder for a `Map` of the values of the HTML input elements.

`validateFromParams(CustomFieldParams params, ErrorCollection errors, FieldConfig config)`

> This is the first method that is called after a user has edited a custom field's value. Any errors recorded here will be nicely displayed next to the field in the edit page.

`getValueFromCustomFieldParams(CustomFieldParams customFieldParams)`

> This method is where a new value for a field that has been accepted by `validate FromParams` is cleaned and converted into a transport object. The `custom FieldParams` object will only contain strings for the HTML elements with a `name` attribute that is the custom field ID—e.g., `customfield_10010`. A null value means that there is no value for this field.

`getStringValueFromCustomFieldParams(CustomFieldParams parameters)`

> This method returns an object that may be a `String`, a `Collection` of `Strings` or even a `CustomFieldParams` object. It's used to populate the `value` variable used in

Velocity templates. It's also used in the `Provider` classes that are used by custom field searchers.

`String getStringFromSingularObject(Carrier singularObject)`
This method is *not* the direct opposite of `getSingularObjectFromString` as you might expect. Instead, it is used to convert a singular object (`Carrier`) to the string that is used in the web page, not to the database value. The returned `String` is also sometimes what is stored in the Lucene indexes for searching ("More Complex Searchers" on page 57). The singular object was passed into this method as an `Object` before JIRA 5.0

The final set of `CustomFieldType` methods to consider are:

`Set<Long> remove(CustomField field)`
This method is called when a custom field is entirely removed from a JIRA instance, and returns the issue ids that were affected by the removal. The correct method to use for deleting a value from a field is `updateValue`.

`String getChangelogValue(CustomField field, Object value)`
`String getChangelogString(CustomField field, Object value)`
These methods are how the text that is seen in the *History* tab of an issue is generated. When a custom field of this type changes, these methods are called with the before and after values of the field. The difference between the two methods is that the if the value later becomes invalid, the string will be shown instead (*https: //developer.atlassian.com/display/JIRADEV/Database+Schema#DatabaseSchema -ChangeHistory*).

`extractTransferObjectFromString()`
`extractStringFromTransferObject()`
These methods are not from the `CustomFieldType` interface but they exist in the standard *Multi* fields for use during project imports.

Other Interfaces

There are a few other interfaces that are commonly implemented by custom field types.

`ProjectImportableCustomField`
The `getProjectImporter` method from this interface is used to implement how the custom field is populated during importing a project from an XML backup. If you don't implement this interface then project imports will not import values for your custom field.

`MultipleCustomFieldType`
`MultipleSettableCustomFieldType`
These two interfaces are used by custom fields with options and that furthermore can have more than one option. For these classes, the values can be accessed using the `Options` class, which is a simple subclass of a Java `List`. These interfaces are not really intended for use by general-purpose multiple value custom field types.

SortableCustomField
> This interface contains a compare method for comparing two singular objects. This is used by the Issue Navigator when you click on a column's heading to sort a page of issues. This is actually a slower fallback for custom fields that don't have a searcher associated with them (see Chapter 4).

RestAwareCustomFieldType RestCustomFieldTypeOperations
> These two interfaces are how the JIRA REST API knows which fields can be retrieved or updated. New in JIRA 5.0

Velocity Templates for Multiple Values

Example 3-8 shows the view Velocity template file for the multiple values custom field type. The Collection of Carrier objects is iterated over and displayed as a table in the issue's web page.

Example 3-8. view.vm for multiple values

```
#if ($value)
  #if ($value.size() > 0)

  <table width="50%">

  <tr width="15%">
    <td>
      Amount
    </td>
    <td>
      Note
    </td>
  </tr>

  #if ($!issue)
    ## issue exists and has a key so the value is a transport of string values,
    ## not a transport object of the singular objects. We want more than just
    ## strings so access the transport object directly from the customfield

    #set ($carriers = $customField.getValue($issue))
  #else
    ## issue does not exist because we are displaying a default value
    ## and so value is a Collection of Carrier objects.

    #set ($carriers = $value)
  #end

  #foreach ($carrier in $carriers)
    <tr>
      <td>
        $!carrier.getAmount()
      </td>

      <td>
        $!carrier.getNote()
```

```
      </td>
    </tr>
  #end

  </table>
  #end
#end
```

The **edit** Velocity resource for the multiple values custom field type is shown in Example 3-9 and is a little more complex. Every HTML element uses the same value in its name attribute and this value is the custom field id such as "customfield_10010". The strings added by a user when editing a field's value arrive at the custom field type in the same order that they appeared in the rendered HTML page.

The **id** attribute for each HTML element should be unique and the built-in **$velocity Count** variable is useful for doing that. The **$velocityCount** variable is incremented each time the **#foreach** Velocity command iterates. The Velocity macros such as *customControlHeader* appear on a single line in the source code for this chapter.

Example 3-9. edit.vm for multiple values
```
#customControlHeader ($action $customField.id \
    $customField.name $fieldLayoutItem.required $displayParameters $auiparams )
<table>
  ### All input elements for this custom field should have a name of
  ## $customField.id but each id should be unique

  #set ($field_uid = $customField.id)

  <tr width="15%">
    <td>
      Amount
    </td>
    <td>
      Note
    </td>
  </tr>

#if ($value)
  #if ($issue.getKey())
    ## issue exists and has a key so the value is a transport of string values,
    ## not a transport object of the singular objects. We want more than just
    ## strings so access the transport object directly from the customfield

    #set ($carriers = $customField.getValue($issue))
  #else
    ## When this template is used to edit a default value then
    ## issue is a dummy with no key. Access the transport object via
    ## the configs variable.

    #set ($carriers = $configs.get("default"))
  #end

  #foreach ($carrier in $carriers)
```

```
    <tr width="15%">
      <td>
        <input id="${field_uid}-amount-${velocityCount}"
               name="${field_uid}"
               type="text"
               value="$carrier.getAmount()" />
      </td>

      <td>
        <input id="${field_uid}-note-${velocityCount}"
               name="${field_uid}"
               type="text"
               value="$textutils.htmlEncode($carrier.getNote())" />
      </td>
    </tr>
  #end

#end

    <tr width="15%">
      <td>
        <input id="${field_uid}-amount-new"
               name="${field_uid}"
               type="text"
               value="" />
      </td>

      <td>
        <input id="${field_uid}-note-new"
               name="${field_uid}"
               type="text"
               value="" />
        Add a new value. Clearing an amount deletes a row.
      </td>
    </tr>
</table>
#customControlFooter ($action $customField.id \
    $fieldLayoutItem.fieldDescription $displayParameters $auiparams )
```

Note that the `edit` Velocity template file is also used when creating a default value, so we can't add help text that only makes sense when editing the field within an issue. There is also a rarely-used `edit-default` Velocity resource that can be used just for editing a default value.

Multiple Values Summary

This section covered some of what is needed to implement a custom field type with multiple values. It also allowed us to describe the purposes of the many methods that are in the `CustomFieldType` interface.

However, custom field types that contain multiple values are definitely harder to implement correctly than ones with single values. Even once the Java methods are defined, working out what is valid in the Velocity context for viewing and editing is not easy. Supporting default values adds to the complexity, and then issue moves and project imports require still more testing. It's not for the fainthearted, but it is doable.

Read-only and Calculated Fields

Even if a field in JIRA does not appear on a create or edit screen, it can still be viewed and also searched on. You can also create fields that are read-only, even if they do appear on create and edit screens.

Creating a read-only JIRA field is fairly straightforward. As described in Chapter 2, a custom field is defined by adding a `customfield-type` to the *atlassian-plugin.xml* file. If there is no `<resource type="velocity" name="edit" />` element within the `customfield-type` element, then nothing will be displayed for that field on an edit screen. You can also use an `#if` condition in a velocity template file, as described in "Velocity Templates for Multiple Values" on page 42, to decide whether or not to display anything for editing. There is also the `readonly` attribute that can be set on any HTML input element to make it read-only. If you do provide an edit screen, make sure the field's value is shown in an `input` element or the field will be cleared when you save other edits to the issue.

A calculated field is a read-only field whose value is derived from elsewhere and doesn't actually store any value in the database. For example, a custom field that displays the number of other issues linked to an issue would calculate that value, likely using the `IssueLinkManager` class. Since that value cannot be changed directly by a user, such a field would either not be displayed in an edit screen or shown as read-only.

There is a convenient abstract class named `CalculatedCFType` that can be extended by a custom field type class. This class conveniently stubs out all the methods that don't need to be implemented by such a class.

A calculated field type class will need to implement the `getValueFromIssue` method to return the calculated value for an issue, which implies choosing a transport object type as well. The other two methods that must be implemented are `getStringFromSingular Object` and `getSingularObjectFromString`. If the class implements the `SortableCustom Field` interface, then the `compare` method will also need to be implemented. Using a `String` as the transport object will make all of this a bit easier.

WebWork

The *WebWork* web application framework is what JIRA uses to map its URLs to the Java classes that produce the HTML for the JIRA web pages. The version of WebWork used by JIRA is a fork from a older version. (Historical information about WebWork can be found at *http://www.opensymphony.com*.) The source can be downloaded from the Subversion repository at *https://svn.atlassian.com/svn/public/atlassian/vendor/web work-1.4/trunk.*

There are lots of other examples of how to use WebWork to add and modify JIRA's web pages in the WebWork Sample plugin (WSMPL) that I wrote. This plugin can be found at *http://marketplace.atlassian.com/17189.*

Other Examples of Custom Field Types

There are many JIRA plugins freely available that contain useful examples of how to create new custom field types. Some of these are listed below. They're also good places to see how some aspects of custom fields work that are not yet covered in this book— e.g., project imports, moving an issue and bulk issue operations.

JIRA Database Values Plugin - https://marketplace.atlassian.com/4969
> This plugin displays values from an external database as strings. It's a good example of extending an existing custom field type (`TextCFType` which is deprecated in 5.0) and adding lots more functionality.

JIRA Suite Utilities - https://marketplace.atlassian.com/5048
> The location-related custom fields described at *https://studio.plugins.atlassian.com/ wiki/display/JSUTIL/JIRA+Suite+Utilities+Custom+Fields* add support for displaying addresses in Google Maps.

JIRA Toolkit - https://marketplace.atlassian.com/5142
> This is one of the earliest plugins from Atlassian and contains many different calculated fields. It's a little dated now since much of its functionality is now part of JIRA, but it is still maintained by Atlassian.

JIRA Enhancer - https://marketplace.atlassian.com/5139
> This plugin contains many calculated fields related to the last time that something happened; a comment, a resolution or a status change.

GreenHopper
> GreenHopper is an Atlassian JIRA plugin that is sold as a separate product. The source code is available to anyone with a non-evaluation license, including the $10 starter licenses. One of the GreenHopper custom field types is the "GreenHopper Ranking" in *RankingCFType.java*, which lets you assign a strict order to issues. While this custom field type is fairly complex, it's also a good example of a fully-implemented and well-tested custom field type from Atlassian.

## CHAPTER 4

Custom Field Searchers

Overview

The previous chapters discussed how custom fields work in JIRA. This chapter covers how searching for values in custom fields works, along with an example of a custom field searcher for the *Currency* custom field type that was created in "A New Custom Field Type" on page 17. All the source code for the examples in this chapter is available from *https://marketplace.atlassian.com/41293*.

When you configure a new custom field in JIRA you specify a name for the field and choose a custom field type. At the same time you can also optionally select a *search template* so that you can search for issues with a given value in the field.

For example, when you add a new custom field of the standard type "Multi Select", the default search template is named "Multi Select Searcher". This searcher is what controls what you see when you're searching for issues in the Custom Fields section of the top-level Issue Navigator page. There may be more than one searcher available for each custom field type. If you select "None" for the searcher, then you won't see any reference to this field in the Issue Navigator search fields.

When creating a new custom field type such as *Currency*, you may well be able to reuse an existing searcher. For example, a custom field type that just formats some text in a different way can probably reuse the "Free Text Searcher" class that's already defined for the standard JIRA *Free Text* custom field type. Alternatively, you may want to create a new searcher and have your new custom field type use that, either using existing Velocity template files or some new templates created just for that searcher. The standard JIRA searchers are defined in *system-customfieldtypes-plugin.xml* in `custom field-searcher` elements.

You can also add a new searcher to an existing custom field type such as "Free Text" or "Select List". This is useful if you want to change how searches on an existing custom field happen. You can't directly change the searchers used for system fields but see "Further Reading" on page 61 for a way to work around this.

Figure 4-1 summarizes the relationship between some of the custom field types and their searchers. The dotted lines indicate searchers that could be used by the custom fields.

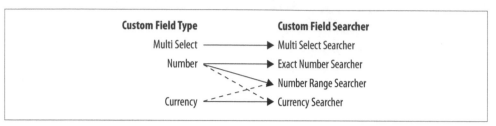

Figure 4-1. Custom Field Types and Searchers

The next section covers some of the underlying mechanisms of how searchers work. An understanding of this is helpful when you come to implement and debug your own custom field searcher, but if you just want to quickly create a searcher for your own custom field type, skip ahead to the examples that start at the section "A Simple Searcher" on page 54.

How Searchers Work

For performance reasons JIRA almost never queries its underlying database directly. Instead, it creates indexes of the necessary data using the popular *Lucene* search tool with one Lucene `Document` object per JIRA issue. These indexes are updated when an issue changes or when the entire Lucene index is rebuilt. JIRA then uses these much faster Lucene indexes to search for the Documents that match a query and then returns the related JIRA issues.

A custom field searcher defines both what should be added to each Lucene Document in the index, and also the Lucene query to run against the index when searching for issues. Searchers also define what appears when results are grouped and the autocompletion prompts used when entering search values.

JIRA has its own query language named *JQL* (JIRA Query Language) which is used to generate these Lucene queries. The JQL syntax resembles the more familiar database query language SQL. You enter constraints in the Issue Navigator simple search screen, for example by selecting the *TEST* project and a status of *Open*. From these constraints JIRA creates a JQL query. The advanced search screen shows the JQL query directly, in this case:

```
project = TEST and status = Open
```

It's worth noting that you can also create plugins that provide new JQL functions for searching both fields and also the rest of JIRA's data. However to change what is stored for each issue you need to use a searcher. See the section "Further Reading" on page 61 for links to more information about this.

Methods for a Custom Field Searcher

JIRA custom field searcher classes extend the base class `AbstractInitialization CustomFieldSearcher`, which has a `CustomFieldSearcherModuleDescriptor` variable that contains the details of how the searcher was defined in *atlassian-plugin.xml*. This descriptor is also used to create the Velocity context, which is used to render how the searcher appears on a web page.

All custom field searchers also implement the `CustomFieldSearcher` interface. This interface and its parent interface `IssueSearcher` have the following methods.

`void init(CustomField field)`
> This is where a searcher gets connected to a specific custom field. The `init` method must set four variables that are used by the other methods. These four variables are:
> - `searcherInformation`
> - `searchInputTransformer`
> - `searchRenderer`
> - `customFieldSearcherClauseHandler`

`getDescriptor()`
> This method returns the `CustomFieldSearcherModuleDescriptor` variable, which is the class that handles creating HTML related to the custom field and the searcher.

`SearcherInformation getSearchInformation()`
> This method returns a `SearcherInformation` object which is used to refer to information about this searcher. That object in turn has a method get `RelatedIndexers` that returns the `FieldIndexer` classes that add this field's data to the Lucene `Document` in an index, as described in "Adding Data to the Lucene Index" on page 50.

`SearchInputTransformer getSearchInputTransformer()`
> This method returns the `SearchInputTransformer` object, which is used to convert the value submitted from the Issue Navigator field to the format used in a `Search Request` for a query. Some of the class names of these transformers are unwieldy— e.g., *AbstractSingleValueCustomFieldSearchInputTransformer.java*.

`SearchRenderer getSearchRenderer()`
> This method returns the `SearchRenderer` object which renders the HTML for the searcher by using the descriptor object. The search renderer uses a `CustomFieldValueProvider` object, which is what calls the `CustomFieldType` methods to get the `$value` object used in a Velocity template.

`CustomFieldSearcherClauseHandler getCustomFieldSearcherClauseHandler()`
> Provides the object that handles the JQL clauses that this searcher creates. These `Clause` objects are eventually converted to a Lucene query. This object is also where the supported operators and data type of the searcher are stored. The `ClauseVa`

`luesGenerator` parameter in the constructor for this object is where the 15 auto-completion values for JQL are created for each field.

Another interface that is implemented by many searchers is `SortableCustomField Searcher` which makes sorting results much faster than just using a custom field's `SortableCustomField` interface. This interface has just one method, which is `getSorter`.

The interface `CustomFieldStattable` is used if you want to be able to use the results from this searcher in gadgets and reports that summarize by a particular custom field. That interface is described in more detail in "Statistical Searchers" on page 59.

Adding Data to the Lucene Index

All kinds of data can be stored in a Lucene index, usually as a string. The value stored corresponds to the value of a custom field, but it could also be a value of a calculated field ("Read-only and Calculated Fields" on page 45) or something else entirely, as shown in the example in "More Complex Searchers" on page 57.

 The value stored in an index only gets updated when an issue is edited. This is usually just fine, except if a calculated field is depending upon values that are not part of that same issue. For example, if a calculated field displays the sum of numbers in fields from three other issues, and one of the values changes, then the stored index value is now out of date and incorrect search results will occur. One approach to solving this is to have a service that updates the index values periodically. Another approach is to use a listener that reindexes specific issues when the values the field depends on changes.

The `FieldIndexer` object that is passed to the `SearcherInformation` constructor is what controls the values that are added to the Lucene index. The `FieldIndexer` object is only used when an issue has been changed, or when the whole Lucene index is being recreated by a JIRA Administrator or a scheduled JIRA job or service.

All `FieldIndexer` classes should extend `AbstractCustomFieldIndexer` which has three methods of interest. The first two methods are abstract and so must be implemented. In most `FieldIndexer` implementations they both call the third method to do the actual indexing work.

`addDocumentFieldsSearchable()`
   This method is called when updating the index for a custom field that is visible in the given issue. The field's value is usually added verbatim to the Lucene index but a modified version may be used instead.

`addDocumentFieldsNotSearchable()`
   This method is called when updating the index for a custom field that is not visible in the given issue, for example if the custom field is not valid in the issue's project.

The value is still added to the Lucene index but is marked as not present in this issue.

addDocumentFields()

This is the main method called by the other two methods to get the field's value from the issue and convert it to a `String` for storing in the Lucene index. The `indexType` parameter is important since it controls what Lucene does to the value before it is added to the index. This is also how more than one value for a field can be stored in given Lucene `Document` as described in "More Complex Searchers" on page 57.

 If you want to see exactly what is in each Document in a Lucene index, download the *Luke* diagnostic tool from *http://code.google.com/p/luke* and run it with:

```
java -jar lukeall-1.0.1.jar
```

Choose any file in *caches/indexes/issues* under your `jira.home` directory, and check the "Open in Read-Only mode" checkbox.

You'll see the Lucene `Fields`, which are the various pieces of information that can be searched on for an issue. The *Documents* tab has arrows that let you see each Lucene Document with the *issue_id* and *key* fields for its JIRA issue. The *Doc. Id* field is the unique id for each Lucene Document.

The *Search* tab lets you choose a default field on the right, add a value on the left, and then click *Search* to see the information about a specific JIRA issue. Or you can just enter *key:TEST-123* on the left and click the Search button. Double-clicking on the result brings up the information about that issue's values in the index.

Executing a Search

When you click the Search button to run a query, the JQL query is parsed to generate an object that implements the `com.atlassian.query.Query` interface. This `Query` object has two main methods: `getWhereClause` and `getOrderByClause`. The names of these methods reflect what a typical SQL *select* statement looks like, for example:

```
select * from jiraissue where project=10100 order by priority
```

A *where* `Clause` object is actually a tree of `Clause` objects that can be combined using the *And*, *Or* and *Not* operators.

The main `SearchService search` method takes a `Query` object and walks down the tree of *where* `Clause` objects to create a Lucene query. The query is executed and the issues that correspond to the resulting Lucene Documents are returned in `SearchResult` object, sorted according to the "order" clause.

The detailed sequence of methods of how all that happens is shown in Figure 4-2.

```
IssueNavigator doExecute()

Retrieve the current SearchRequest object and get the JQL Query object from it

executeSearch() then calls getSearchResults()

LuceneSearchProvider search() is run as the current user and calls getHits() with
a desired range of issues

LuceneSearchProvider getHits() creates a Lucene Query from the JQL query

LuceneSearchProvider runSearch() queries the Lucene "issues" index using the search()
method in org.apache.lucene.search.Searcher

For each Lucene Document that was matched, the JIRA issue is added to the SearchResult
that is eventually returned.
```

Figure 4-2. Executing a search

 You can display the original JQL query and its associated Lucene query
in the JIRA log file by adding the following lines to *log4j.properties* file:

```
log4j.logger.com.atlassian.jira.issue.search.providers.LuceneSearchProvider = \
    INFO, console, filelog
log4j.additivity.com.atlassian.jira.issue.search.providers.LuceneSearchProvider
    = false
```

The creation of a Lucene Query from a JQL *where* `Clause` is done by the `createLucene
Query` method in the `DefaultLuceneQueryBuilder` class. This method walks down the
tree of clauses, building up the Lucene Query as it goes and handling negation and
empty clauses.

The JQL Clauses used for each specific custom field are found via the `create
AssociatedSearchHandler` method in the `CustomFieldImpl` class. This method returns a
`SearchHandler` object, which is another container of information about the searcher.

Searchers and atlassian-plugin.xml

Getting the `customfield-searcher` element for custom field searchers right in *atlassian-
plugin.xml* is a confusing area, so this section covers it in some detail before we come
to the examples. The JIRA documentation for the `customfield-searcher` plugin module
type can be found at *https://developer.atlassian.com/display/JIRADEV/Custom+Field
+Plugin+Module*, but it is somewhat sparse.

The various elements and attributes used when defining a `customfield-searcher` element in *atlassian-plugin.xml* are as follows.

key
> The identifier for the searcher, unique within this plugin. This is typically some-
> thing like "mycustomfield-searcher". If this is changed later on you wont' be able

to use the searcher in a field until you edit the field and choose the searcher with the new key.

name
description

> The name is a short string that is displayed when a JIRA administrator chooses this searcher while creating or editing a custom field. For example, "Free Text Searcher". The description string only appears in the list of a plugin's modules. These can both be changed at any time.

class

> This is the Java class that actually implements the searcher. This may be a class that extends one of the system searcher classes that are listed in *system-custom-fieldtypes-plugin.xml*. It could also be a plugin class that's a totally new searcher.

resource

> These elements refer to the Velocity template files that the searcher should use. The search resource controls how the search field appears in the Issue Navigator. The view resource controls how a search constraint is displayed in the *Summary* tab of the Issue Navigator. The label resource, if present, is used to control how statistics about the results are shown.

> The resource's files can be ones shipped with JIRA under *atlassian-jira/WEB-INF/classes/templates/plugins/fields* or files that are part of the searcher plugin. You can use your own searcher with JIRA's existing Velocity templates, or you can use your own template files with extended instances of existing JIRA searcher classes—or a mixture of the two.

valid-customfieldtype

> These elements control which custom fields this searcher can be used with. The package and key attributes are easy to get wrong, and then your custom field won't have the expected searcher choices available for it.

> The key attribute has to be exactly the same as the key attribute of the desired customfield-type element.

> The package attribute has to be the same as the key attribute of the custom field's top-level atlassian-plugin element. For system searchers this key is com.atlassian.jira.plugin.system.customfieldtypes. For custom fields the key is defined (by default) using the Maven variables like this:

```
<atlassian-plugin
    key="${project.groupId}.${project.artifactId}"
    name="${project.artifactId}"
    plugins-version="2">
```

For the example in Chapter 2, the valid-customfieldtype package would be com.mycompany.jira.plugins plus a period plus currency (i.e., com.mycompany .jira.plugins.currency). Note that this package attribute is a string, *not* a Java class or package name.

A Simple Searcher

The first searcher example is a searcher for the *Currency* custom field type that was created in "A New Custom Field Type" on page 17. This custom field type displays a number according to the local currency conventions.

The class for the custom field type extends the standard `NumberCFType` class so we can reuse and extend one of the searchers that are already defined for that class in *system-customfieldtypes-plugin.xml*.

To do this, find the `customfield-type` element for the `NumberCFType` custom field type class and note the value of its `key` element. In this case the value is "float". Now search in the same file for `customfield-searcher` elements with `valid-customfield-type` elements that have a `key` attribute of `float`. This produces the two searchers that *Number Field* custom fields can use: *NumberRangeSearch* and *ExactNumberSearcher*. We'll use the latter class in this example. "Exact" means that no pattern matching such as 10* is supported by the searcher.

 You can tell whether an existing searcher will work with a particular custom field type if the searcher class uses a `FieldIndexer` class that refers to objects of the same class as the custom field type's transport object (see "Fields with Multiple Values" on page 38).

In an ideal world, we would just declare a similar `customfield-searcher` element in the Currency plugin's existing *atlassian-plugin.xml* using the same `ExactNumberSearcher` searcher class, and then declare the new `customfield-searcher` as valid for the Currency custom field type. Example 4-1 shows the new searcher in the same *atlassian-plugin.xml* file that was shown in Example 2-1.

Example 4-1. atlassian-plugin.xml with a searcher added

```
<customfield-searcher key="currencysearcher"
                      name="Currency Searcher"
                      class="com.mycompany.jira.plugins.currency.searchers.
                          CurrencySearcher"> ❶
    <description>
        Allow searching for a currency value.
    </description>

    <resource type="velocity" ❷
              name="search" ❸
              location="templates/com/mycompany/jira/plugins/currency/searchers/
                  search.vm"/>
    <resource type="velocity"
              name="view" ❹
              location="templates/com/mycompany/jira/plugins/currency/searchers/
                  summary.vm"/>
```

```
<valid-customfield-type package="com.mycompany.jira.plugins.currency"
                        key="currency-field"/> ❺
</customfield-searcher>
```

❶ This is the class of the custom searcher we are creating. A separate Java package name for searcher classes is generally a good idea.

❷ These are copies of the Velocity template files that the existing `ExactNumber Searcher` uses in the *Number Searcher* searcher.

❸ The search resource is what controls the HTML input field for this searcher in the Issue Navigator.

❹ The view resource defines what appears for the searcher in the Issue Navigator's *Summary* tab.

❺ Make sure we get the `package` and `key` right for the custom field type that we want to search, as noted in "Searchers and atlassian-plugin.xml" on page 52. The custom field is defined in the same *atlassian-plugin.xml* file as the searcher.

The main difference from an ideal world is that the existing `ExactNumberSearcher` searcher class can't be referred to directly by the `customfield-searcher` element because it's not part of the plugin. To work around this we create a new class in the plugin whose sole purpose is to act as a wrapper for that searcher class. Since the searcher class is intended for the *Currency* field type, we'll call it `CurrencySearcher`. It is shown in full in Example 4-2.

Example 4-2. CurrencySearcher.java

```java
package com.mycompany.jira.plugins.searchers.currency;

import com.atlassian.jira.issue.customfields.converters.DoubleConverter;
import com.atlassian.jira.issue.customfields.searchers.ExactNumberSearcher;
import com.atlassian.jira.issue.customfields.searchers.transformer.CustomFieldInputHelper;
import com.atlassian.jira.jql.operand.JqlOperandResolver;
import com.atlassian.jira.util.I18nHelper;
import com.atlassian.jira.web.FieldVisibilityManager;

/**
 * A custom searcher class that simply reuses an existing searcher.
 */
public class CurrencySearcher extends ExactNumberSearcher {

    public CurrencySearcher(final FieldVisibilityManager fieldVisibilityManager,
                            final JqlOperandResolver jqlOperandResolver,
                            final DoubleConverter doubleConverter,
                            final CustomFieldInputHelper customFieldInputHelper,
                            final I18nHelper.BeanFactory beanFactory) {
        super(fieldVisibilityManager,
              jqlOperandResolver,
              doubleConverter,
              customFieldInputHelper,
              beanFactory);
```

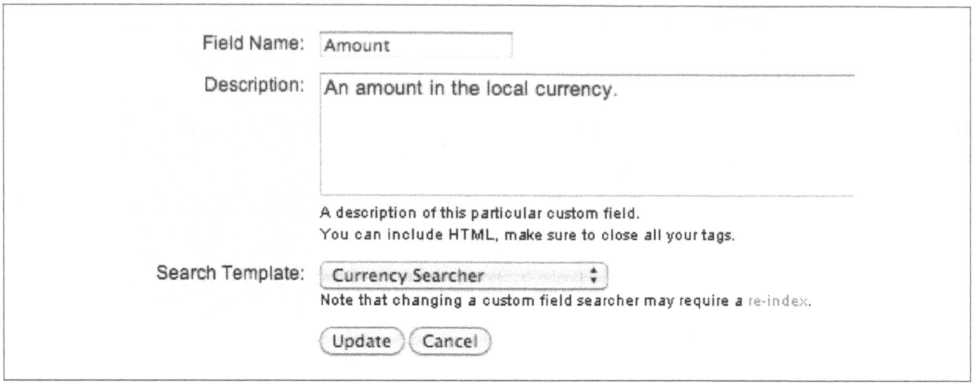

Figure 4-3. Using the new searcher in a custom field

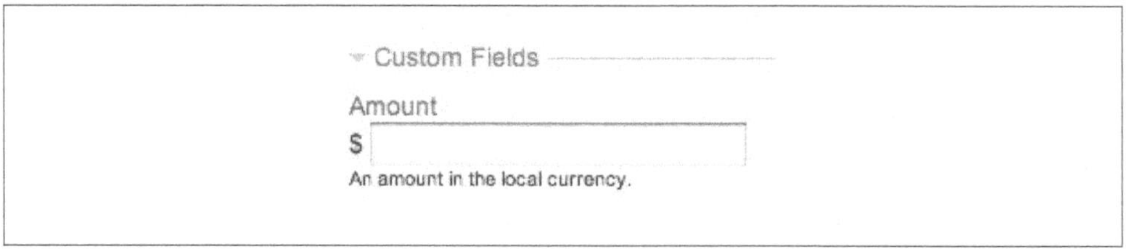

Figure 4-4. The new searcher in the Issue Navigator

```
    }

}
```

The `search.vm` and `summary.vm` Velocity resources in *atlassian-plugin.xml* are copies of the template files used by the *Number Field* custom field with changes to add the currency symbol, just as described in "Adding Velocity Template Files" on page 22.

Once we have rebuilt and redeployed the plugin, we should see the new searcher as a module in the *Currency* plugin details in the Administration→Plugins page. We can also now change the search template used for a Currency custom field to the new *Currency Searcher* searcher by using the *Edit* link, as shown in Figure 4-3.

After reindexing, the custom field should duly appear in the Custom Fields section of the Issue Navigator as shown in Figure 4-4, which is very similar in appearance to editing a Currency value shown in Figure 2-2. Searching for a number should find all issues that contain that number. And because we extended a standard searcher we can even use other operators such as < and >.

Troubleshooting Searchers

If the searcher doesn't appear in as a choice in a custom field's *Edit* screen, check the log file for any ERROR or WARN strings associated with loading the plugin. The searcher should appear as a valid and enabled module of the plugin at the Administration→Plugins page.

If the searcher still doesn't appear as a choice, it may be that the `valid-customfield type` element is incorrect, as discussed in the section "Searchers and atlassian-plugin.xml" on page 52.

If you're developing a new custom searcher and you're not getting the results you expect, reindex and check what's actually in the Lucene index by using the `luke` tool described in "Methods for a Custom Field Searcher" on page 49. Increasing the logging of the `LuceneSearchProvider` class as described in "Executing a Search" on page 51 can also help.

More Complex Searchers

This next example shows how we can create more complex searchers. For the first example we're going to change what is stored in the Lucene index for the Currency custom field type. We'll add the string `Small` to the Lucene index for all values less than 10, so we can easily find all the issues with small amounts in a *Currency* field.

The searcher class to extend for this example is `AbstractInitializationCustomField Searcher`, which is also the parent class of most of the existing searchers. The easiest way to do this is to copy the contents of the *ExactNumberSearcher.java* source file to a new file named *CurrencyAdvancedSearcher.java* and make sure that it compiles in your plugin environment. You'll probably need to add some `import` statements for a few classes that are in the original searcher's package.

All the work in a custom field searcher is done in the `init` method, where the four main variables listed in "Methods for a Custom Field Searcher" on page 49 are set. What gets complicated is that each of these variables is created with a non-trivial number of other variables. Thankfully, most of the time only a few of these variables need to be changed.

The way that data is stored in the Lucene index is controlled by a `FieldIndexer` object in the searcher class. We can replace the `NumberCustomFieldIndexer` object that the original `ExactNumberSearcher` used with a new indexer object of class `CurrencyCustom FieldIndexer`. In our example this is the line in *CurrencyAdvancedSearcher.java* that looks like this:

```
final FieldIndexer indexer =
  new CurrencyCustomFieldIndexer(fieldVisibilityManager, field,
      doubleConverter);
```

The changes in the new `CurrencyCustomFieldIndexer` class are shown in Example 4-3. We have modified the `addDocumentFields` method to add another value to the `Document` object in the Lucene index when the field has a value less than 10. It's fine to have multiple entries in the Document for the same custom field id in the same issue. The entries are more like labels or tags than unique identifiers.

Example 4-3. Changes to CurrencyCustomFieldIndexer.java

```java
package com.mycompany.jira.plugins.currency.searchers;

import com.atlassian.jira.issue.index.indexers.impl.AbstractCustomFieldIndexer;
import com.atlassian.jira.issue.Issue;
import com.atlassian.jira.issue.customfields.converters.DoubleConverter;
import com.atlassian.jira.issue.fields.CustomField;
import static com.atlassian.jira.util.dbc.Assertions.notNull;
import com.atlassian.jira.web.FieldVisibilityManager;

import org.apache.lucene.document.Document;
import org.apache.lucene.document.Field;

/**
 * A custom field indexer for Currency custom fields
 */
public class CurrencyCustomFieldIndexer extends AbstractCustomFieldIndexer {

    public final static String SMALL = "Small";


    // addDocumentsFieldsSearchable, addDocumentsFieldsNotSearchable methods
    // omitted for space

    private void addDocumentFields(final Document doc,
                                   final Issue issue,
                                   final Field.Index indexType) {
        Object value = customField.getValue(issue);
        if (value == null) {
            return;
        }
        Double dbl = (Double)value;

        final String stringValue = doubleConverter.getStringForLucene(dbl);
        // This is a Lucene Field, not a JIRA CustomField
        Field field = new Field(getDocumentFieldId(),
                                stringValue,
                                Field.Store.YES,
                                indexType);
        doc.add(field);

        // Add the extra information to the index
        if (dbl.doubleValue() < 10.0) {
            field = new Field(getDocumentFieldId(),
                              SMALL,
                              Field.Store.YES,
                              indexType);
            doc.add(field);
        }
    }
```

}

Now after a reindex, the Lucene index will have two values for this custom field for each issue. However because one of the values is a text string instead of a number string, we also need to change how the search input is validated.

When a value is entered in the search field in the Issue Navigator, it is validated and converted to a transport object by the custom field methods, as discussed in "Custom-FieldType Methods" on page 39. This means that to make the string "Small" acceptable as a search term, we have to update the getSingularObjectFromString method in the CurrencyCFType custom field type of "A New Custom Field Type" on page 17. The change is shown in Example 4-4. Another file *CurrencyIndexValueConverter.java* also has to be changed slightly to handle a string (see the source code).

Example 4-4. Changes to CurrencyCFType.java

```
public Double getSingularObjectFromString(String numberString)
    throws FieldValidationException {

    // This is for the advanced currency searcher
    if (numberString.equalsIgnoreCase(CurrencyCustomFieldIndexer.SMALL)) {
        return Double.valueOf("0");
    }

    // code omitted for brevity
}
```

The case-insensitive string "Small" is now accepted as a valid value for a Currency custom field and can be used by the searcher.

 Some FieldIndexer classes store the value field's value and also a modified value that is more useful for searching or sorting. For example, *Select List* options are indexed both by the raw value and also by a string with all upper-case characters converted to lower-case to make searching for an option independent of its case.

Statistical Searchers

JIRA has many gadgets and reports that allow you to summarize the number of issues by the different values in a field. For example, you can use the *Issue Statistics* gadget to display a histogram of the number of issues in each status. To make this possible with a custom field instead of status, the searcher for that field must implement the Custom FieldStattable interface.

The CustomFieldStattable interface has just one method: getStatisticsMapper. Most searcher classes can usually just return one of the classes that already implement the StatisticsMapper interface, or you can create a new class. The important thing is to choose a `StatisticsMapper` class that expects the data in the Lucene index to be the same kind of data that the searcher's `FieldIndexer` added to the index. The `getSorter` method defined in the `SortableCustomFieldSearcher` interface often returns the same `StatisticsMapper` object as the `getStatisticsMapper` method.

Within a `StatisticsMapper` class, the `getDocumentConstant` method must return the value that the field was indexed with, usually the `customfield_NNNNN` field ID. The `getValueFromLuceneField` method should return an Object that is of the same type as the custom field's singular object and one that works with the `Comparator` returned by the `getComparator` method.

We can easily modify *CurrencySearcher.java* and make it implement `CustomFieldStattable` by reusing the existing `NumericFieldStatisticsMapper` class, as shown in Example 4-5. Only the changes from Example 4-2 are shown, and in the source code this searcher's file is named *CurrencyStattableSearcher.java*

Example 4-5. A Stattable searcher

```
import com.atlassian.jira.issue.customfields.statistics.CustomFieldStattable;
import com.atlassian.jira.issue.statistics.NumericFieldStatisticsMapper;
import com.atlassian.jira.issue.statistics.StatisticsMapper;

public class CurrencySearcher extends ExactNumberSearcher
                        implements CustomFieldStattable {



    public StatisticsMapper getStatisticsMapper(final CustomField customField) {
        return new NumericFieldStatisticsMapper(customField.getId());
    }

}
```

However no names for the field's values will appear in our gadgets unless we add a suitable `label` resource in *atlassian-plugin.xml*, as shown in Example 4-6. Adding new variables to the Velocity context for the `label` resource is not a simple matter, but the `customField` variable can be used to access the `CustomFieldType` object and its `get VelocityParameters` method. That's one way to access the `numberTool` object so the correct currency symbol can be displayed in the label.

Example 4-6. A label resource in atlassian-plugin.xml

```
<resource type="velocity"
          name="label"
          location="templates/com/mycompany/jira/plugins/currency/searchers/label.vm" />
```

After deploying this new searcher, edit a *Currency* custom field and select the new "Stattable Currency Searcher". After reindexing, the custom field should now appear as a selection in the lists of fields that you can summarize results by in the *Issue Statis-*

tics gadget. The resulting histogram is shown in Figure 4-5. If you don't reindex you may get errors or incorrect values displayed.

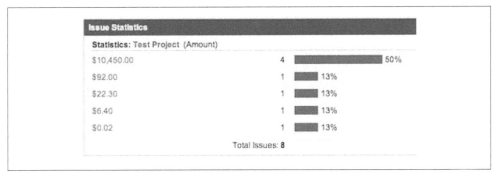

Figure 4-5. Custom field searcher statistics in a gadget

Further Reading

One plugin that demonstrates how to extend a system searcher class is the *JIRA Searchable Attachments* plugin (*https://marketplace.atlassian.com/4868*). Even though its latest release is for JIRA 3.x, the code works fine with JIRA 4.3.

Another JIRA plugin that implements a custom searcher is the *JIRA Mobile Connect* plugin, available at *https://bitbucket.org/atlassian/jiraconnect-jiraplugin*. This plugin uses a `Location` singular object that records the longitude and latitude of the device from which a user provided feedback.

The main page for the Apache Lucene project is *http://lucene.apache.org*. There is an excellent book "Lucene in Action" by Erik Hatcher, Otis Gospodnetic, and Michael McCandless (Manning), with a web page and a couple sample chapters available at *http://www.manning.com/hatcher3*. Make sure you get the second edition (July 2010), since it covers the versions of Lucene used by recent JIRA releases.

There is an brief overview of how JQL works at *https://confluence.atlassian.com/display/JIRA/_Searching+in+JIRA*. A good starting point for learning more about JQL plugins is *https://developer.atlassian.com/display/JIRADEV/Plugin+Tutorial+-+Adding+a +JQL+Function+to+JIRA*. The *HP/Palm Jira Search* plugin at *https://marketplace.atlassian.com/plugin/details/338080* has many examples of reasonably complex JQL functions.

As mentioned earlier, you can't change the searcher for JIRA system fields directly but you can achieve the same result by creating a new calculated custom field type (see "Read-only and Calculated Fields" on page 45) that just returns the value of the system field. Then create a new searcher for that calculated custom field. You can also make the calculated custom field type invisible in issues by not providing any Velocity resources for it, and just use it for searching.

## CHAPTER 5

Workflow Customizations

Overview

This chapter covers how to create JIRA plugins for use with workflows. Conditions, validators and post-functions are each described in detail, with both nonconfigurable and configurable examples. All the source code for the examples in this chapter is available from *https://marketplace.atlassian.com/41293*. The standard JIRA conditions, validators, and post-functions plugins are also useful examples and can be found in the file *system-workflow-plugin.xml*.

Conditions

Conditions control whether a transition appears in a user's list of available workflow actions. For instance, the default JIRA workflow only shows the *Start Progress* transition to the current assignee of an issue. Other users don't see the transition as a choice in their view of the issue's actions.

Conditions are configured with the *Add* link on the *Conditions* tab of a workflow transition, as described at *http://confluence.atlassian.com/display/JIRA/Configuring+Work flow#ConfiguringWorkflow-Addingacondition*. You can also combine multiple conditions using AND and OR operations, but not negation.

Creating a custom condition is relatively straightforward, at least compared with custom fields and searchers. The first example is of a condition that has no configuration.

First we add a workflow-condition element to *atlassian-plugin.xml* as shown in Example 5-1.

Example 5-1. atlassian-plugin.xml for a condition with no configuration

```
<workflow-condition key="custom-noconfig-condition"
        name="A Custom Condition With No Configuration" ❶
        class="com.mycompany.jira.plugins.workflow.WorkflowNoInputConditionFactoryImpl"> ❷
```

```
<description>
  A condition with no configuration.
</description>

<condition-class>
  com.mycompany.jira.plugins.conditions.ConditionNoConfig  ❸
</condition-class>

<resource type="velocity"
          name="view"  ❹
          location="templates/com/mycompany/jira/plugins/conditions/
              condition-view.vm"/>
</workflow-condition>
```

❶ The name of the condition as it appears when you add a condition to a transition, along with the contents of the description element.

❷ The Java class that is used to configure the condition.

❸ The Java class that actually implements the condition.

❹ This Velocity template contains the text for the condition, in this case "This text comes from the view Velocity resource". That text is what is seen when adding the new condition, as shown in Figure 5-1.

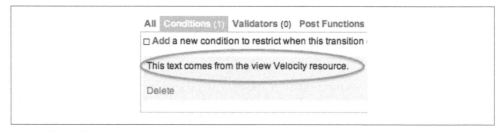

Figure 5-1. Adding a new condition, showing the text from the view template file

Next we need a Java class to control how the condition is configured. Since there is nothing to configure for this condition, we can use the simple `WorkflowNoInput ConditionFactoryImpl` class shown in Example 5-2. Most of the system classes that implement the `WorkflowPluginConditionFactory` interface look like this.

Example 5-2. WorkflowNoInputConditionFactoryImpl.java

```java
package com.mycompany.jira.plugin.workflow;

import com.opensymphony.workflow.loader.AbstractDescriptor;
import com.atlassian.jira.plugin.workflow.WorkflowPluginConditionFactory;
import java.util.Map;
import java.util.HashMap;
import java.util.Collections;

public class WorkflowNoInputConditionFactoryImpl
          implements WorkflowPluginConditionFactory {
```

```
    // This controls what appears in the Velocity context for viewing
    // the condition
    public Map getVelocityParams(String resourceName,
                                 AbstractDescriptor descriptor) {
        // This is empty because we don't need any variables in the
        // Velocity context as we are not configuring the condition
        return new HashMap();
    }

    // This controls what is passed in the args parameter of the
    // passesCondition method of the ConditionNoConfig class
    public Map getDescriptorParams(Map conditionParams) {
        // This is empty because there is no configuration
        return Collections.EMPTY_MAP;
    }
}
```

Then we create the Java source file *ConditionNoConfig.java* that actually implements the condition and is shown in Example 5-3. The parent class `AbstractJiraCondition` is the class that custom conditions should extend, since it provides the useful methods `getCaller` and `getIssue`.

Example 5-3. ConditionNoConfig.java, a condition with no configuration

```
package com.mycompany.jira.plugins.conditions;

import com.atlassian.crowd.embedded.api.User;
import com.atlassian.jira.exception.DataAccessException;
import com.atlassian.jira.issue.Issue;
import com.atlassian.jira.workflow.condition.AbstractJiraCondition;
import com.opensymphony.module.propertyset.PropertySet;
import com.opensymphony.workflow.WorkflowException;
import java.util.Map;
import org.apache.log4j.Logger;

public class ConditionNoConfig extends AbstractJiraCondition {
    private static final Logger log = Logger.getLogger(ConditionNoConfig.class);

    /**
     * @param transientVars a Map of key/value pairs populated by the
        Factory class for this condition
     * @param args and ps used for configurable conditions
     *
     * @return true if the condition passes for the current user
     */
    public boolean passesCondition(Map transientVars,
                                   Map args,
                                   PropertySet ps) throws WorkflowException {
        log.debug("Checking the noconfig condition");

        // This is the user who is viewing the issue that has this transition
        User user = getCaller(transientVars, args);
```

```
        try {
            Issue issue = getIssue(transientVars);
            // More logic would usually go here
            return true;
        } catch (DataAccessException e) {
            log.warn("Failed to find the expected issue", e);
        }
        return false;
    }

}
```

After the plugin has been built and deployed to JIRA, the custom condition should appear as a choice when adding a new condition to a transition in a workflow. When the workflow has been published, then the transition should always appear as a choice in an issue since passesCondition always returns true in this example.

Configurable Conditions

Now let's make the same custom condition configurable. The good news is that the way that this is done for conditions is the same way that configuration is added to validators and post-functions.

To provide support for configuration, we have to add two more Velocity resources (input-parameters and edit-parameters) to *atlassian-plugin.xml*, as shown in Example 5-4. The difference between the two resources is that input-parameters is used when defining the configuration for a *new* condition, whereas the edit-parameters resource is used for editing the configuration of an *existing* condition.

Example 5-4. Adding more resource elements in atlassian-plugin.xml

```
<workflow-condition key="custom-config-condition"
      name="A Custom Condition With Configuration"
      class="com.mycompany.jira.plugins.workflow.WorkflowWithInputConditionFactoryImpl">

    <description>
      A condition that also has some configuration.
    </description>

    <condition-class>
      com.mycompany.jira.plugins.conditions.ConditionWithConfig
    </condition-class>

    <resource type="velocity"
              name="view"
              location="templates/com/mycompany/jira/plugins/conditions/condition-view-
                  config.vm"/>
    <resource type="velocity"
              name="input-parameters"
              location="templates/com/mycompany/jira/plugins/conditions/condition-
                  edit.vm"/>
```

```
<resource type="velocity"
          name="edit-parameters"
          location="templates/com/mycompany/jira/plugins/conditions/condition-
              edit.vm"/>
</workflow-condition>
```

In this example, both of the new resources can use the same template file *condition-edit.vm*, as shown in Example 5-5. This file contains an HTML text input element with a `name` attribute (not an `id` attribute) of `mycurrentvalue`.

Example 5-5. condition-edit.vm

```
## The same Velocity template file is used by the input-parameters and
## edit-parameters resources in this example.
<tr>
  <td>
    <input type="text" name="mycurrentvalue" value="$!mycurrentvalue"/>
  </td>
</tr>
```

This new Velocity template file expects the `mycurrentvalue` variable to have been added to the Velocity context that was used to render it. This is done in the `WorkflowWith InputConditionFactoryImpl` class, as shown in Example 5-6. The single `getVelocity Params` method of the earlier `WorkflowNoInputConditionFactoryImpl` class is replaced by three `getVelocityParamsFor` methods: one for each of the Velocity resources (`view`, `input-parameters`, and `edit-parameters`). So `getVelocityParamsForInput` is only called when no existing configuration exists and `getVelocityParamsForEdit` is called when there is an existing configuration value. An example of the sort of thing that could be added to the `edit-parameters` and `input-parameters` Velocity contexts by these methods is a `Collection` of values to populate an HTML select element in the Velocity template file.

The `ConditionDescriptor` object is what represents the underlying OSWorkflow Condition. This descriptor has a `Map` that can be used to contain various parameters used by the condition. Custom configuration values such as `mycurrentvalue` can be added to this Map using the `getDescriptorParams` method in `WorkflowWithInputCondition FactoryImpl`. Example 5-6 shows this method.

Example 5-6. WorkflowWithInputConditionFactoryImpl.java

```
package com.mycompany.jira.plugins.workflow;

import com.opensymphony.workflow.loader.AbstractDescriptor;
import com.opensymphony.workflow.loader.ConditionDescriptor;
import com.atlassian.jira.plugin.workflow.WorkflowPluginConditionFactory;
import com.atlassian.jira.plugin.workflow.AbstractWorkflowPluginFactory;
import com.atlassian.core.util.map.EasyMap;

import java.util.Map;
import java.util.HashMap;
import java.util.Collections;
```

```
public class WorkflowWithInputConditionFactoryImpl
    extends AbstractWorkflowPluginFactory
    implements WorkflowPluginConditionFactory {


    /**
     * @param A set of parameters from the web page.
     * @return a Map of values that is passed into the passesCondition
     * method and is also available via descriptor.getArgs()
     */
    public Map getDescriptorParams(Map conditionParams) {
        // Read the one parameter we care about from the condition-edit
        // velocity template
        String value = extractSingleParam(conditionParams, "mycurrentvalue"); ❶

        // passesCondition will look for this key in its args variable
        return EasyMap.build("mycurrentvalue", value); ❷
    }

    protected void getVelocityParamsForView(Map velocityParams,
                                            AbstractDescriptor descriptor) {
        if (!(descriptor instanceof ConditionDescriptor)) {
 throw new IllegalArgumentException("Descriptor must be a ConditionDescriptor");
        }

        ConditionDescriptor conditionDescriptor = \
                        (ConditionDescriptor) descriptor;
        String value = \
            (String) conditionDescriptor.getArgs().get("mycurrentvalue");
        if (value == null) {
            value = "Not yet set";
        }
        velocityParams.put("mycurrentvalue", value);
    }

    protected void getVelocityParamsForInput(Map velocityParams) {
        // Text fields don't need any other parameters
    }

    protected void getVelocityParamsForEdit(Map velocityParams,
                                            AbstractDescriptor descriptor) {
        getVelocityParamsForInput(velocityParams);
        getVelocityParamsForView(velocityParams, descriptor);
    }
```

❶ The parameter name matches the name of the HTML element in *condition-edit.vm*.

❷ The name of the key for the Map matches the string used to access the value in passesCondition.

Since the configuration is stored with the descriptor, this also means that the get VelocityParamsForView method can extract the value from conditionDescriptor to add it to the Velocity context for viewing the current configuration.

Finally, we can use the configuration within the `passesCondition` method of the class `ConditionWithConfig` that actually implements the condition. Example 5-7 shows the configuration parameter being used as a version name so that only issues with a given *Fix Version* will display the transition as a workflow choice for users.

Example 5-7. ConditionWithConfig.java, a condition with configuration

```
public boolean passesCondition(Map transientVars,
                               Map args,
                               PropertySet ps) throws WorkflowException {
    log.debug("Checking the condition");

    try {
        String configparam = (String) args.get("mycurrentvalue");
        log.debug("This condition was configured with a value: " + configparam);
        if (configparam == null) {
            // If the condition was not configured, it isn't active
            return true;
        }

        // As an example only show the workflow transition if the
        // issue has a Fix Version that matches the configured
        // value by name.
        Issue issue = getIssue(transientVars);
        Collection<Version> versions = issue.getFixVersions();
        for (Version version: versions) {
            if (version.getName().equals(configparam)) {
                return true;
            }
        }
        return false;
    } catch (DataAccessException e) {
        log.warn("Failed to find the expected issue in the database");
    }
    return false;
}
```

To test the custom condition, add the new condition to a transition and publish the workflow. If the condition doesn't appear as a choice to be added, check the JIRA log file for errors about loading the custom workflow plugin. If the condition is already present and the plugin fails to load, then JIRA just shows the classname of the condition but the condition is inactive.

Next, view a suitable issue. The transition shouldn't be offered as a choice unless the condition was configured with some string. Finally, the issue's *Fix Versions* have to include one version whose name matches the string that was configured for this condition.

Validators

A validator controls whether a transition's screen contains acceptable values. What's the difference between a condition and a validator? A condition is tested before a transition is permitted, whereas a validator is tested after the transition screen inputs have been entered.

In this section, we will create a custom validator that requires that a date in a field is in the future. The example assumes that there is a *Date Picker* custom field named "Future Date Field" and that the field appears on the screen of the transition that the validator is added to.

As shown in Example 5-8, the *atlassian-plugin.xml* file for a validator plugin is very similar to that for a condition. The Java class named in the `class` attribute for the configuration factory has to implement the interface `WorkflowPluginValidatorFactory` instead of `WorkflowPluginConditionFactory` (even though they are both empty interfaces). Otherwise, the factory for a validator with no configuration is identical to one for a condition with no configuration that was shown in Example 5-2.

Example 5-8. atlassian-plugin.xml for a validator with no configuration

```
<workflow-validator key="custom-noconfig-validator"
        name="A Custom Validator With No Configuration"
        class="com.mycompany.jira.plugins.workflow.WorkflowNoInputValidatorFactoryImpl">

    <description>
      A validator with no configuration to check that a date
      field is not in the past.
    </description>

    <validator-class>
      com.mycompany.jira.plugins.validators.ValidatorNoConfig
    </validator-class>

    <resource type="velocity"
                name="view"
                location="templates/com/mycompany/jira/plugins/validators/validator-
                    view.vm"/>
  </workflow-validator>
```

The `validator-class` element has to refer to a class such as the one shown in Example 5-9 which implements the OSWorkflow `Validator` interface directly, since there is no equivalent of the `AbstractJiraCondition` class for validators. The values entered by the user during the transition are present in the `Issue` object named "issue" in the `transientVars` variable.

Example 5-9. ValidatorNoConfig.java, a validator with no configuration

```java
/**
 * A validator with no configuration to check that a date is not in the past.
 * Failure to validate throws an InvalidInputException.
 */
public class ValidatorNoConfig implements Validator
{
    public void validate(Map transientVars,
                         Map args,
                         PropertySet ps) throws InvalidInputException {
        try {
            // Get the issue as modified in the transition screen
            Issue issue = (Issue) transientVars.get("issue");

            // Get the date value from a hard-coded field name
            String fieldName = "Future Date Field";
            CustomField cf =
    ManagerFactory.getCustomFieldManager().getCustomFieldObjectByName(fieldName);
            if (cf == null) {
                throw new InvalidInputException(
    "The validator failed to find the date custom field: " + fieldName);
            }

            // This will use the default value, if any
            Date value = (Date) issue.getCustomFieldValue(cf);
            if (value == null) {
                // The field was not set or was not present in the
                // transition screen
                return;
            }
            log.debug("The modified issue has a custom field value of : " + value);

            // Check that the date is in not in the past. Today is not
            // valid either.
            Date today = new Date();
            if (value.compareTo(today) < 0) {
                throw new InvalidInputException(
    "The validator failed because the date " + value + " is in the past");
            }
        } catch (DataAccessException e) {
            throw new InvalidInputException(
    "The validator failed to validate because it could not find the issue");
        }
    }
}
```

The `validate` method in the `Validator` interface is very similar to the `passesCondition` method of `AbstractJiraCondition`. One difference is that if the validation fails, an `InvalidInputException` is thrown instead of returning a boolean `false` as a condition does. The text in such an exception is neatly displayed to the user as a "Workflow Error" if there is no transition screen. There is also a two-argument constructor for `InvalidInputException` that can be used to display groups of errors. However, the entire stack trace of a failed validation is also dumped into the JIRA log file, which is a bit distracting for JIRA administrators.

Configurable Validators

The way that configuration is added to validators is almost identical to how it was added to conditions in "Configurable Conditions" on page 66. There is a different factory class `WorkflowWithInputValidatorFactoryImpl` that is used in *atlassian-plugin.xml*, but the factory class implements the same three `getVelocityParamsFor` methods and stores the configuration value in the descriptor's `Map` just like the condition's factory does.

The class `ValidatorWithConfig` which actually implements the `Validator` interface retrieves the configured parameter from the `args` parameter, just as the `ConditionWith Config` class does. The values entered by the user in a transition screen are present in the `Issue` object named "issue" in the `transientVars` variable as usual.

The only other difference is the lack of an `AbstractJiraValidator` class for validators. That means that if you want to access the original issue, as it was before the transition screen, you have to cut and paste the `getIssue` method from `AbstractJiraCondition`.

Post-Functions

Post-functions are actions that happen after a transition. JIRA automatically adds a number of them to every transition to do things such as reindex the issue, add a change log entry, and fire an event. You can use custom post-functions to update an issue in many different ways, but our example will simply add a new line of text to the issue's description.

First we add a `workflow-function` element to *atlassian-plugin.xml*, as shown in Example 5-10. This is very similar to the changes to *atlassian-plugin.xml* in Example 5-1 for conditions and Example 5-8 for validators.

Example 5-10. atlassian-plugin.xml for a post-function with no configuration

```
<workflow-function key="postfunction-noconfig"
      name="A Custom Post-function with No Configuration"
      class="com.atlassian.jira.plugin.workflow.WorkflowNoInputPluginFactory"> ❶
  <description>
    A custom post-function with no configuration.
  </description>

  <function-class>
    com.mycompany.jira.plugins.functions.FunctionNoConfig ❷
  </function-class>

  <!-- "The weight and default parameters for workflow functions
        should not be used by plugin authors and should be considered
```

```
            reserved for JIRA's use." -->
   <orderable>true</orderable> ❸
   <unique>false</unique> ❹
   <deletable>true</deletable> ❺

   <resource type="velocity"
             name="view"
             location="templates/com/mycompany/jira/plugins/functions/function-view.vm"/>
</workflow-function>
```

❶ There is already a convenient factory class `WorkflowNoInputPluginFactory` from Atlassian for post-functions that don't have any configuration.

❷ The class that implements the post-function.

❸ If true, then the order of the post-function can be changed. The top post function as displayed is the one that is executed first during a transition.

❹ If true, then only one instance of the post-function can appear in each transition.

❺ If true, then the post-function can be deleted from the transition.

The post-function custom class `FunctionNoConfig` shown in Example 5-11 extends the `AbstractJiraFunctionProvider` class, which has a convenient method `getIssue` for accessing the issue as it was before the transition occurred. The `execute` method is the analog of the `passesCondition` and `validate` methods used by conditions and validators. It also takes the same three parameters as those other methods do.

Example 5-11. FunctionNoConfig.java, a Post-function with no configuration

```java
package com.mycompany.jira.plugins.functions;

import com.atlassian.jira.issue.MutableIssue;
import com.atlassian.jira.workflow.function.issue.AbstractJiraFunctionProvider;
import com.opensymphony.module.propertyset.PropertySet;
import com.opensymphony.workflow.WorkflowException;
import org.apache.log4j.Logger;
import java.util.Map;
import java.util.Date;
import java.util.Iterator;

public class FunctionNoConfig extends AbstractJiraFunctionProvider {

    private static final Logger log = Logger.getLogger(FunctionNoConfig.class);

    public void execute(Map transientVars,
                        Map args,
                        PropertySet ps) throws WorkflowException {
        log.debug("The post-function is ready to do something");

        MutableIssue issue = getIssue(transientVars);

        String description = issue.getDescription();
        if (description == null) {
            description = "";
```

```
        }

        if (description.length() > 512) {
            // This is displayed on a screen as a Workflow Error
            throw new WorkflowException("The description text is longer than
                512 characters");
        }

        issue.setDescription(description + "\nPost-function called at " + new Date());
    }
}
```

A post-function makes changes to the current issue by modifying the issue retrieved using the getIssue method.

 If you are using a post-function to update the issue, then you may have to make sure that your post-function appears first in the list of post-functions, or at least before the *reindex* post-function.

One instance when post-functions are awkward to use is when they are added to the *Create* transition for an issue. The originalissueobject and issue objects in the transientVars variable don't exist yet. However, you can still access the underlying HttpServletRequest object and see all the inputs in that way, as the execute method does in the EditConfiguration class shown in Example 3-7.

If an error occurs within the execute method of a post-function, you can throw a WorkflowException. This exception will be caught and displayed on the transition screen if it exists, or on a special *Workflow Error* screen if there is no screen associated with the transition. However, the stack trace is still dumped into the JIRA log either way.

Configurable Post-Functions

Adding configuration to a post-function is almost exactly the same as adding configuration to a condition or validator, as described in the section "Configurable Conditions" on page 66.

The factory class should implement the WorkflowPluginFunctionFactory interface, which has the same three getVelocityParamsFor methods and stores the configuration value in the function descriptor's Map just as before.

Further Reading

The main page in the Atlassian documentation for the topics covered in this chapter is *https://developer.atlassian.com/display/JIRADEV/How+to+create+Custom+Workflow +Elements+for+JIRA+3.x*, but it's somewhat dated (as its title indicates).

Another place to start is with the API documentation for the various plugin modules related to workflow customization at *https://developer.atlassian.com/display/JIRADEV/Workflow+Plugin+Modules*.

The JIRA Misc Workflow Extensions (JMWE) plugin from Innovalog at *https://marketplace.atlassian.com/292* contains good examples of custom conditions, validators, and post-functions.

Fidel Castro Armario's JIRA Workflow Toolbox plugin at *https://marketplace.atlassian.com/29496* has lots of examples of what can be done in workflows, though it is a closed source product.

There are also useful blog posts about creating a custom validator, a post-function, and a condition at *http://www.j-tricks.com/1/post/2010/08/workflow-validator.html*, *http://www.j-tricks.com/1/post/2010/08/workflow-post-function.html* and *http://www.j-tricks.com/1/post/2010/08/workflow-condition.html*.

The source code for the underlying `com.opensymphony.workflow` OSWorkflow libraries that are used by JIRA workflows can be downloaded from *https://maven.atlassian.com/content/repositories/atlassian-3rdparty/opensymphony/osworkflow/2.8.0/osworkflow-2.8.0-sources.jar*

## CHAPTER 6

Storing Data with Your Plugin

Overview

One of the most common questions when adding new functionality to JIRA is "where do I store my plugin's data?". The brute-force way is to add new tables or new columns to the database by modifying the file *entitydefs/entitymodel.xml*, but then all your future upgrades will need to make the same changes.

Two better approaches to storing your data are covered in this chapter. The first one is to use the same PropertySet interface that JIRA uses for much of its own configuration data. The second approach is to use the newer Active Objects plugin, which can handle both more complex data and more of it. This Atlassian plugin is shipped as part of JIRA 5.0 and later, but can also be installed separately in JIRA 4.3 and 4.4.

Storing Data with PropertySet

The first approach is to store plugin data where JIRA stores this kind of configuration data, which is in the propertyentry table. This also has the advantage of allowing us to use the same classes, such as PropertyUtils, that JIRA uses for accessing the data. However it is strictly key/value pairs with no idea of relational concepts.

The way that JIRA uses the propertyentry database table is based on the PropertySet interface from OpenSymphony. This interface allows you to store unique "key=value" pairs with various get and set methods for different types of data.

The propertyentry table is defined in the *entitymodel.xml* file, as shown in Example 6-1. Note that the entity name OSPropertyEntry is the name that JIRA uses internally when referring to the propertyentry database table.

Example 6-1. OSPropertyEntry as defined in entitymodel.xml

```
<entity entity-name="OSPropertyEntry"
        table-name="propertyentry"
        package-name="">
    <field name="id" type="numeric"/>
```

```
        <field name="entityName" type="long-varchar"/>
        <field name="entityId" type="numeric"/>
        <field name="propertyKey" type="long-varchar"/>
        <field name="type" col-name="propertytype" type="integer"/>
        <prim-key field="id"/>
    </entity>
```

We can also examine the resulting **propertyentry** table and its fields using the MySQL command line tool. Other databases' tools should show similar output with different names for the types, but don't assume that the name of a table or field or maximum field lengths are the same when using a different database.

```
mysql> describe propertyentry;
+--------------+---------------+
| Field        | Type          |
+--------------+---------------+
| ID           | decimal(18,0) |
| ENTITY_NAME  | varchar(255)  |
| ENTITY_ID    | decimal(18,0) |
| PROPERTY_KEY | varchar(255)  |
| propertytype | decimal(9,0)  |
+--------------+---------------+
```

The purpose of each field in the **propertyentry** table is as follows:

ID
> A unique identifier for every piece of configuration data

ENTITY_NAME
> The class name of the data object being stored

ENTITY_ID
> Identifies a specific instance of the data object

PROPERTY_KEY
> The key of the *key=value* pair

propertytype
> The data type of the value—e.g., 5 for a string

For each **propertytype**, the corresponding table where the actual value of the data is stored is:

```
1 for propertynumber
5 for propertystring
6 for propertytext
```

The **propertystring** table looks like this in *entitymodel.xml* and MySQL.

```
<entity entity-name="OSPropertyString"
        table-name="propertystring"
        package-name="">
    <field name="id" type="numeric"/>
    <field name="value" col-name="propertyvalue" type="very-long"/>
    <prim-key field="id"/>
```

```
</entity>

mysql> desc propertystring;
+---------------+---------------+------+-----+---------+-------+
| Field         | Type          | Null | Key | Default | Extra |
+---------------+---------------+------+-----+---------+-------+
| ID            | decimal(18,0) | NO   | PRI | NULL    |       |
| propertyvalue | text          | YES  |     | NULL    |       |
+---------------+---------------+------+-----+---------+-------+
```

An Example of Storing Data

Understanding **propertyentry** is much easier with a concrete example. Let's say I want to store two street addresses. In XML, they might look something like this:

```
<address id="10010" housenumber="10" street="Oak Avenue" city="San Jose">
<address id="10200" housenumber="32" street="Long Street" city="London">
```

In the **propertyentry** table, the data would look like this:

```
ID   ENTITY_NAME   ENTITY_ID   PROPERTY_KEY    PROPERTYTYPE

100  Address       10010       House_Number    5
101  Address       10010       Street          5
102  Address       10010       City            5

103  Address       10200       House_Number    5
104  Address       10200       Street          5
105  Address       10200       City            5
```

First, the ID column is a unique identifier for every piece of data in this table.

Then, the entity name **Address** is the kind of data we want to store. In an Object Relational Model (ORM), this is the class name of the object being stored.

Then comes the entity ID, which distinguishes multiple addresses from each other. In an ORM, this is a unique identifier for each instance of an object.

Then the property key contains the name of a data field within each address. This is the "key" part of the "key=value" pair that is being stored.

There's one last field in the **propertyentry** table: **propertytype**. The most common value is 5, which means that the value is a string less than 255 characters long and is stored in the **propertystring** table. A value of 1 is for boolean settings such as enabling or disabling voting and its value is stored in the **propertynumber** table. A value of 6 is for larger blocks of text such as the license data and is stored in **propertytext**.

The values in the **propertystring** table for our example would be:

```
ID    PROPERTYVALUE

100   10
101   Oak Avenue
102   San Jose
```

```
103   32
104   Long Street
105   London
```

The ID field in this secondary table is the ID of each entry in the **propertyentry** table. The **propertyvalue** is the "value" part of the "key=value" pair that is being stored for that row in **propertyentry**.

Accessing the Data

We first have to create a **PropertySet** object that knows how to refer to just one address, say the one with an entity ID value of 10010. Some sample code to create a **Property Set** object is shown in Example 6-2.

Example 6-2. Creating a PropertySet

```
import com.opensymphony.module.propertyset.PropertySet;
import com.opensymphony.module.propertyset.PropertySetManager;

protected PropertySet getPS(long entityId) {
    HashMap ofbizArgs = new HashMap();
    ofbizArgs.put("delegator.name", "default");
    ofbizArgs.put("entityName", "Address");
    ofbizArgs.put("entityId", new Long(entityId));
    ofbizPs = PropertySetManager.getInstance("ofbiz", ofbizArgs);
    return ofbizPs;
}
```

We can now store a value using a **PropertySet** object with code such as:

```
PropertySet propertySet = getPS(10010);
propertySet.setString("Street", "Pine Avenue");
```

This will update one row in the underlying **propertystring** table so that it looks like this:

```
ID    PROPERTYVALUE
101   Pine Avenue
```

A similar method can be used to retrieve data using a **PropertySet** object:

```
String currentStreet = propertySet.getString("Street");
```

Most plugins create a separate Data Access Object (DAO) class to handle working with **PropertySet** objects and the underlying database. For a block of configuration data, a unique entity name can be created and the same entity ID can be reused. In this case the entity ID can be chosen at random.

Further Examples and Resources

JIRA's internal user properties are stored with a property key prefixed by `jira.meta.`, so if you store a user property "hair_color=brown" for a particular user whose ID is 10000, then you will see an entry in **propertyentry** that looks like:

```
mysql> select * from propertyentry where property_key like 'jira.meta%';
+-------+-------------+-----------+-----------------------+--------------+
| ID    | ENTITY_NAME | ENTITY_ID | PROPERTY_KEY          | propertytype |
+-------+-------------+-----------+-----------------------+--------------+
| 10111 | OSUser      |     10000 | jira.meta.hair_color  |            5 |
+-------+-------------+-----------+-----------------------+--------------+
```

and an entry in **propertystring** such as

```
mysql> select * from propertystring where id=10111;
+-------+---------------+
| ID    | propertyvalue |
+-------+---------------+
| 10111 | brown         |
+-------+---------------+
```

As of JIRA 5.1, many plugins still store their configuration data using **PropertySet** though plenty are moving to Active Objects. The Atlassian Shared Access Layer (SAL) provides a general class named **PluginSettings** that can be used by all Atlassian plugins for storage. In the case of JIRA, it's just a thin layer over **PropertySet**. A little more information about this can be found at *http://blogs.atlassian.com/2009/01/post_1/*.

One example of a plugin that uses **PropertySet** in a more complex way than usual is the JIRA Create and Link plugin (*https://studio.plugins.atlassian.com/source/browse/ JCLP*), which stores its configuration as an XML string in the **propertyentry** table.

The PropertySet Storage Toolkit plugin from Leonid Maslov at *https://marketplace.at lassian.com/34011* contains wrapper classes for accessing data stored in a Property Set. This plugin is a little dated but still a good example.

Storing Data with Active Objects

The second, newer approach to storing plugin data is to use Active Objects (AO). AO is an ORM project based at *http://java.net/projects/activeobjects*. The Atlassian Active Objects plugin builds on this to make it fit with the way plugins work in JIRA and Confluence. This approach promises to be easier to use for larger amounts of data and also to scale better than **PropertySet** storage.

There is some excellent documentation for Active Objects at *https://developer.atlassian .com/display/AO/Active+Objects*, particularly the "Getting Started" page, so this section is just a brief overview of how to use AO.

The main idea is to define a Java interface that extends the AO **Entity** interface, as shown in Example 6-3. An entity is the same concept as it is in a *PropertySet*; i.e., it is the class of the object to be stored. The underlying fields are defined by creating **get** and **set** methods in the interface.

Example 6-3. Defining an Entity subinterface in Address.java

```
package com.mycompany.jira.plugins.aoexample;

import net.java.ao.Entity;

public interface Address extends Entity {
    String getHousenumber();
    void   setHousenumber(String housenumber);

    String getStreet();
    void   setStreet(String street);

    String getCity();
    void   setCity(String city);
}
```

The type of the object used in the get and set methods could have been a boolean or a more complex class, itself defined as an AO interface. There are also annotations available to make the relationship between entities one to many, or many to many. AO supports real relationships, not just key/value pairs like PropertySet.

To use AO in JIRA we need to refer to it in the Maven *pom.xml*, as shown in Example 6-4. If this isn't present, then the plugin build will fail to find the AO classes (see "Troubleshooting a Build" on page 9).

Example 6-4. pom.xml

```
<dependency>
  <groupId>com.atlassian.activeobjects</groupId>
  <artifactId>activeobjects-plugin</artifactId>
  <version>0.19.7</version>
  <scope>provided</scope>
</dependency>
```

We also have to add an ao plugin module element to the *atlassian-plugin.xml* file, as shown in Example 6-5. This tells JIRA which interface class should be mapped to a database table. There can be multiple ao elements in one plugin. A component-import element is also added so that the constructor in Example 6-6 can have an Active Objects object injected into it.

Example 6-5. atlassian-plugin.xml for Active Objects

```
<ao key="address-ao">
  <description>The AO interface for storing Address objects.</description>
  <entity>com.mycompany.jira.plugins.aoexample.Address</entity>
</ao>

<component-import key="ao" name="Active Objects components"
        interface="com.atlassian.activeobjects.external.ActiveObjects">
  <description>Access to the Active Objects service</description>
</component-import>
```

Accessing the Data

This section shows how AO can be used for the usual database operations of inserting, selecting, and updating a row. Example 6-6 shows how a new **Address** object is created and values are added to its fields. The **save** method is what persists the data. If a field is not set when the **Address** object is saved, then it is simply stored as a NULL. All objects that extend the AO **Entity** interface have an underlying integer ID to uniquely identify them.

Example 6-6. Inserting a row using Active Objects

```
package com.mycompany.jira.plugins.aoexample;

import com.atlassian.activeobjects.external.ActiveObjects;;

public class AOExample {

    private final ActiveObjects ao;

    public AOExample(ActiveObjects ao) {
        this.ao = ao;
    }

    // Create a new instance of the entity
    public void create() {
        Address address = ao.create(Address.class);
        address.setHousenumber("10");
        address.setStreet("Oak Avenue");
        address.setCity("San Jose");
        address.save();
    }

}
```

After the entity has been created, the automatically created database table will look something like this in MySQL:

```
mysql> desc AO_A6C866_ADDRESS;
+-------------+--------------+------+-----+---------+----------------+
| Field       | Type         | Null | Key | Default | Extra          |
+-------------+--------------+------+-----+---------+----------------+
| CITY        | varchar(255) | YES  |     | NULL    |                |
| HOUSENUMBER | varchar(255) | YES  |     | NULL    |                |
| ID          | int(10)      | NO   | PRI | NULL    | auto_increment |
| STREET      | varchar(255) | YES  |     | NULL    |                |
+-------------+--------------+------+-----+---------+----------------+


mysql> select * from AO_A6C866_ADDRESS;
+----------+-------------+----+------------+
| CITY     | HOUSENUMBER | ID | STREET     |
+----------+-------------+----+------------+
| San Jose | 10          |  1 | Oak Avenue |
+----------+-------------+----+------------+
```

The next snippet shows how to select a specific **Address** object, either by its ID or by using a **Query** that resembles a traditional SQL **select** statement.

```
import net.java.ao.Query;

int desiredId = 123;
Address otherAddress = ao.get(Address.class, desiredId);

// We can also use a Query for multiple rows
Address[] addresses = ao.find(Address.class,
                              Query.select().where("city= ?", "San Jose"));
```

Updating an **Address** object is also straightforward:

```
Address address = ao.get(Address.class, desiredId);
address.setCity("Cambridge");
address.save();
```

There is also a **@Transactional** annotation that can be added to AO interfaces to make their methods all operate within a transaction for thread safety.

Further Reading

There is a blog post at *http://www.j-tricks.com/1/post/2012/07/active-objects-injection .html* about how to make sure that the ActiveObjects component is available for your plugin.

OpenSymphony was a long-running project that produced many of the libraries used internally by JIRA. Some of them were forked by Atlassian for their own use. The source code for PropertySet can be found at *https://maven.atlassian.com/content/repositories/ atlassian-3rdparty/opensymphony/propertyset/1.5/propertyset-1.5-sources.The.* jar original source for **PropertySet** can also still be found at *http://svn.opensymphony.com/ svn/propertyset/trunk*.

The JIRA database schema (*https://developer.atlassian.com/display/JIRADEV/Database +is*) Schema defined using the Apache OfBiz Entity Engine and configured with the files in the *entitydefs* directory. More information about how that configuration works can be found at *http://ofbiz.apache.org/docs/entity.html*.

## CHAPTER 7

Publishing Your Plugin

Overview

There are hundreds of public plugins and other add-ons available for JIRA and the other Atlassian tools, all discoverable through the *Atlassian Marketplace* website at *https://marketplace.atlassian.com*. This site was formerly known as "p.a.c." or "PAC" for "plugins.atlassian.com". This is the place to search for new plugins to use in your JIRA, examples to learn from, and where the information about each plugin is published. This chapter describes the Marketplace and its sister sites SPAC and bitbuckct. It also covers the details of upgrading a plugin, both building it and uploading it to the Marketplace The Atlassian developer documentation for the Marketplace can be found at *https://developer.atlassian.com/display/MARKET/Atlassian+Marketplace*.

Atlassian Marketplace

The Atlassian Marketplace is where JIRA's Universal Plugin Manager (UPM) goes to search for plugins. The compatibility information about each plugin at the Marketplace is used to decide which plugins can be installed in a particular version of JIRA. Maintaining the compatibility information for a plugin is important, as plugins can drop out of use fairly quickly if not marked as being compatible with the latest JIRA version.

What the Marketplace offers for each plugin is:

- A top-level summary of the plugin and a summary of each version of the plugin
- The all-important JIRA version compatibility information
- Links for downloading the plugin package
- Links to source code, documentation, and issue tracking
- Screenshots of the plugin in JIRA
- Reviews of the plugin by other users and a history of downloads
- Support contact details, if any

- Support for evaluation licenses
- A convenient way to purchase commercial plugin licenses, and also for vendors to receive 75 percent of the income.

Since the Marketplace is the top-most area of the JIRA plugins community, it is designed to work with many different approaches to writing plugins. It deliberately does not offer anywhere to directly check in source code, track issues, or download plugin packages. Instead, you can use any URL you like for all of those things. Many plugin developers choose to use SPAC, bitbucket or another project hosting service such as `code.google.com` or `sourceforge.net`.

Anyone can search the Marketplace for plugins anonymously, but to publish a plugin, you have to log in using the same account details as your `my.atlassian.com` account. That's the account from which JIRA licenses are downloaded. Each plugin is associated with a *vendor*, which can be a company, organization, or individual. After you log in, there is a *Create new add-on* link on the Manage Add-ons link, which in turn takes you to a link for creating a new vendor. If this is your first plugin, then simply create a new vendor for yourself. If the vendor of the plugin already exists, then you should contact *developer-relations@atlassian.com* to have your user name added to the list of people who publish plugins as that vendor.

SPAC (studio.plugins.atlassian.com)

 Many plugins still are developed using SPAC but new projects are no longer begin accepted. The page at *https://developer.atlassian.com/display/DOCS/Hosting+Options+for+Add-on+Developers* has more information about other choices such as bitbucket and Atlassian's cloud service OnDemand.

SPAC is an instance of JIRA Studio that offers the other parts of a plugin development environment. SPAC is a no-cost location for checking in and browsing source code, tracking issues related to a plugin, and storing plugin documentation. It's also where the actual plugin packages can be stored. Users only have to actually log into SPAC if they want to modify information, comment on the wiki pages, or build the plugin using Bamboo.

For version control, SPAC offers a Subversion repository complete with *trunk*, *branches*, and *tags* directories, with a slightly simplified FishEye instance for browsing the source code. Issue tracking for each plugin is a JIRA project (what else?) and there is a Confluence space for the documentation.

There are two common ways to refer to a particular plugin's package for downloading in the Binary URL section of a PAC plugin version: a FishEye URL or a Confluence attachment URL. Either way the package file has to be downloadable anonymously or the plugin manager in JIRA won't be able to install it.

Using a FishEye URL is the more precise of the two options. It uses the "raw" `https` URL to locate the file in FishEye, e.g., `https://studio.plugins.atlassian.com/source/browse/~raw,r=160160/PRNT/releases/ParentSummaryField-4.3.0.jar` for the plugin PRNT. If you want to update a release, you have to change the URL, but that's fine since it's usually better practice to create a new .jar file and plugin version anyway.

The second way is to upload the plugin package to a Confluence page as an attachment and then use the URL for the attachment, e.g., `https://studio.plugins.atlassian.com/wiki/download/attachments/4085063370/myplugin-1.0.1.jar`. This has the advantage that the source tree in SPAC can then have restricted access (you can email Atlassian with this request) but a plugin's users can still download the plugin and see the documentation. Be aware that if you upload a new file with the same name, the URL does not change.

SPAC also provides builds using Bamboo and code reviews using Crucible. Just contact `developer-relations@atlassian.com` to ask for this to be enabled. In fact, Bamboo provides a third way to distribute a plugin package by using the URL of the build artifact, assuming that the artifact is not subsequently deleted.

bitbucket

bitbucket (*http://bitbucket.org*) is an Atlassian-owned hosting site for the distributed version control systems Mercurial and Git. You can create a public repository for your plugin, or use a private repository for a commercial plugin. Each repository has its own basic wiki and bug tracker.

Upgrading a Plugin to a New Version of JIRA

A new version of JIRA is released a few times each year, and plugins are marked as compatible or not on the Marketplace. Just as when you upgrade JIRA, it's worth having a plan for how you upgrade the plugins that you are using or have developed.

As described in Chapter 1, the JIRA version that a plugin was last built for is defined in the `jira.version` element in its *pom.xml* file. The first thing to do is to check that the plugin still compiles cleanly for that version. Why wouldn't it? Well, Maven downloads the files that are listed in the **dependency** elements and if they are no longer available, and you don't already have them cached on your local machine, the plugin build can fail.

If the plugin fails to build because a Maven repository has removed some old files, you may still be able to build with later versions of the dependencies, though it is rather concerning not having a working base to start from. You may also still be able to find the required .jar files and add them locally, as directed by the Maven build's error messages.

Once you have a working build, you can change the `jira.version` to the new version of JIRA. This value is usually just the major and minor version numbers, e.g., `4.3`. The next build will download the new dependency files, including the new JIRA .jar file, and compile the plugin against them.

It is possible to leave the `jira.version` unchanged and just try deploying the plugin to the new version of JIRA unchanged. However, this means that any errors happen at run-time, which is usually harder to debug. I recommend building using the latest version of JIRA and then testing that plugin for compatibility in older versions.

If the plugin builds cleanly with the new version of JIRA, it will also have compiled and run any unit tests. Passing the unit tests is the first level of upgrading the plugin. If there aren't any unit tests and you add some, then the next time you upgrade you'll be more comfortable at this stage of the upgrade process. There are some further references to testing plugins at *https://developer.atlassian.com/display/DOCS/Plugin+Testing+Re sources+and+Discussion.*

The next step is to deploy the plugin. Whether this is a manual deployment or is done with *atlas-run*, the log file output is the next thing to check. Search for the strings `ERROR` and `WARN`, and see whether any of them are related to the plugin. A plugin can fail when it is loaded at plugin system initialization time (e.g., `UnsatisfiedDependency Exception`), or it can fail the first time something in JIRA uses it, usually with `Lazy LoadedReference` errors.

Each plugin has a unique key defined in *atlassian-plugin.xml*. Don't change this key during an upgrade or any existing JIRA data that used the older version of the plugin won't recognize the newer plugin as being the same one.

Now check the behavior and appearance of the plugin is as expected. If the plugin has integration tests, they can often be invoked with *atlas-integration-test*. In fact, this command is the real way to achieve repeatable and efficient plugin upgrades. With good integration tests, you can change the `jira.version`, run *atlas-integration-test*, and finish this part of an upgrade in minutes.

You can build a plugin for different versions of JIRA either by branching the source code or by using a different *pom.xml* file for each version and the maven `--file` argument. Just be careful to remove the `target` directory between builds.

Updating a Plugin Version at the Marketplace

Once you have a new plugin package ready to distribute, you'll need to create a new version at the Marketplace for it. This process to do that can be confusing the first few times you do it, so this section describes it in detail.

First, log in to the Marketplace as a user associated with the vendor for the plugin. Go to *Manage Add-ons* and click on the plugin for which you wish to release a new version. The *Edit Version* link here is for changing the existing version's details, not for adding a new version.

In the *Versions* section, there is an *Add version* link. The new version page has a space to enter the version number, which should have three digits, or three digits and a string, i.e., "1.2.0" or "1.2.0-beta".

There is also a field named "Build Number" which has to be any number that increases for each different version of the plugin. It could be your local build number but doesn't have to be.

The *plugin system version* is likely to be TWO unless you have a good reason to build an older-style plugin. The differences between them are covered briefly in "Version One, Version Two and Version Three Plugins" on page 95.

The "Binary URL" field for where to download the plugin package from is discussed in "SPAC (studio.plugins.atlassian.com)" on page 86. You can use any URL here.

The "Product Compatibility" field has an Add button that you have to remember to click to save your JIRA version compatibility choices.

Each plugin version can have two values for its status. A DRAFT status means that the plugin version is not visible to other users. A PUBLISHED status means that the version is visible in the list of versions for this plugin. You can have multiple versions of a plugin available at the same time. The Version History section of a plugin's page allows a user to click on a version and then the Download button will change to download the chosen version. The default version of a plugin is the latest one.

Once you have entered all this information, and a plugin version has been created and published, it's worth testing that everything is as expected. To do that, go back to the *Version History* section, click on the new version and check that the *Download* button actually downloads the file that you expected.

Further Reading

The documentation for Marketplace licensing can be found at *http://www.atlassian .com/licensing/marketplace*.

Issues about the Marketplace itself are tracked at *https://ecosystem.atlassian.net/browse/ AMKT*, with some older issues at *https://studio.atlassian.com/browse/PAC*.

## CHAPTER 8

Further Plugin Information

Overview

This chapter covers topics that were more advanced than was appropriate for Chapter 1, or just didn't fit neatly into any other chapter.

JIRA Plugins—Beyond the .jar file

Most JIRA plugins are deployed as a single `.jar` file that contains all the class files, Velocity template files, and other resources needed by the plugin. However, some plugins require other JIRA files to be created or modified at deployment time. These plugins will likely require a restart of JIRA for the changes to take effect.

Some of the kinds of changes that can require these extra steps are:

.jsp files

JSP files are a more complex alternative to Velocity template files and are used for many core JIRA web pages. Some plugins may want to use a copy of such a file with minor changes, rather than rewriting the template using Velocity.

System .xml files

For example, adding new email templates for custom JIRA events may require changes to the *upgrade-system-event-types.xml* file.

System .java files

Some plugins may even expect recompilation of modified JIRA source files in addition to deploying the plugin's .jar file. For example, the standard JIRA Listener for email is always added when JIRA is restarted, unless the code that does this is modified. So custom Email Listener plugins will want to make that small change and recompile the JIRA source file.

Modifying any of the JIRA default Manager classes is another example of where small changes are sometimes easier to make in a single source file. Overriding the classes provided by the JIRA `ComponentManager` class is not always easy.

The simplest way to recompile a JIRA source file is to use the *external-source* subdirectory in the JIRA data directory and the *Ant* build tool.

 When creating JIRA plugins, I always want them to be deployable as one or more `.jar` files. It's makes future upgrades easier and is just more elegant.

Internationalization

Internationalization or "i18n" is the ability to customize JIRA for a specific language and country. For JIRA plugins, this mostly means translations of text strings. For JIRA itself, this work is coordinated by Atlassian at *https://translations.atlassian.com*, but each plugin handles the translation work itself. However, JIRA plugins support i18n the same way that JIRA itself does, by using the underlying `.properties` files that contain the translations, as shown in Example 8-1 and Example 8-2.

Example 8-1. Example of an English .properties file

```
# This is a comment in a properties file
myplugin.name = My Example Plugin
```

Example 8-2. Example of a French .properties file

```
myplugin.name = Mon Exemple Plugin
```

For a plugin to be able to use a properties file, there has to be an `i18n` resource defined in the *atlassian-plugin.xml* file, as shown in Example 8-3.

Example 8-3. i18n in atlassian-plugin.xml

```
<resource type="i18n"
          name="my_plugin_i18n" ❶
          location="com.mycompany.jira.plugins.i18n.en_US" /> ❷
```

❶ This can be any name unique within the *atlassian-plugin.xml* file.

❷ The full name of the properties file is the plugin *src/main/resources* directory plus the `location` value with periods replaced by directory separators and `.properties` appended—i.e., *src/main/resources/com/mycompany/jira/plugins/i18n/en_US.properties*.

I've used a filename of *en_US.properties* here to indicate that the translation in the file is for American English locales. However, the filename can be anything with the `.properties` suffix.

Many of the different plugin module types in JIRA, such as `customfield-type`, have an attribute named `i18n-name-key` that is used by system plugins to internationalize the name of the plugin. That part doesn't seem to work as well for plugins not shipped with JIRA though.

 Plugins developed for JIRA 5.0 and later or for multiple products should follow the approach described in *https://developer.atlassian.com/display/JIRADEV/Plugin+Tutorial+-+Internationalising+Your+Plugin* which uses a servlet and template renderer approach. This approach also supports i18n for JavaScript.

Example 8-4 shows an example of using text from a properties file in a Velocity template. The `i18n` variable is an instance of the `I18nBean` class populated with the relevant properties. If the property key is not found, then the raw key is displayed instead.

Example 8-4. Partly internationalized text in a Velocity template file

```
This plugin's name is $i18n.getText('mplugin.name')
```

You may also want to access text properties from within a plugin's Java source code. This is typically used for translating error messages. The best approach is to obtain a reference to the same `i18n` object used in the Velocity context. Custom fields have a `getI18nBean` method that can be used for this, or a `JiraAuthenticationContext` object can be used to access the object. The `getText` methods that are available in some plugin classes that extend `JiraActionSupport` will only contain the properties defined for JIRA itself.

If all else fails, with JIRA 4.2 and earlier you can access the plugin descriptor directly as shown in Example 8-5. The important part is to use the plugin's class loader for the plugin, not JIRA's default class loader.

Example 8-5. i18n within a plugin's source code

```
// pluginKey is your atlassian-plugin element's key attribute
Plugin plugin = ComponentManager.getInstance().getPluginAccessor().getEnabledPlugin
    (pluginKey);
if (plugin == null) {
    throw new Exception("Unable to find an enabled plugin with the key " + pluginKey);
}

// Access the i18n resource in the plugin by name
ResourceDescriptor plugin_i18n_resource =
    plugin.getResourceDescriptor("i18n", "my_plugin_i18n");
if (plugin_i18n_resource == null) {
    throw new Exception("Unable to find the plugin i18n resource");
}

plugin_i18n = new I18nBean(authenticationContext.getUser(),
                    plugin_i18n_resource.getLocation(),
                    plugin.getClassLoader());
```

```
// This is a translated string
log.info(plugin_18n.getText("plugin.example.message"));
```

Localizing most plugins for a particular country and language currently requires modifying the i18n resource in the *atlassian-plugin.xml* file and repackaging the plugin. However, the Atlassian gadget plugins have a getMessage method that detects the current user's locale and chooses the correct translation based on that, as documented at *https://developer.atlassian.com/display/JIRADEV/Plugin+Tutorial+-+Writing+Gadgets+for+JIRA*. Since Atlassian Gadgets are based on Google's gadgets, there is still further information about this approach at *http://code.google.com/apis/gadgets/docs/i18n.html*.

Plugin Security

JIRA plugins allow you to circumvent most of JIRA's security measures if you want to. So before you install a plugin, check that you either have access to the source code or that you trust the plugin vendor. It also helps to read all the public comments and issues that relate to the plugin at marketplace.atlassian.com and elsewhere.

What's most commonly wanted from a plugin is to preserve the same level of security that is provided by JIRA. This usually requires some minor but explicit actions on the part of a plugin developer.

Some considerations to keep in mind for authentication and authorization include:

- Is there a user currently logged in? Some issue operations such as changing an issue's status will require this.
- Is the current user a member of a group or in a certain project role? For instance, only members of the *jira-administrators* group should see the JIRA administration pages.
- Does the current user have a particular permission that is needed for an action? For instance, JIRA Administrators may be part of the JIRA Administrators group or the JIRA System Administrators group, and both groups may have to be checked.
- Cross-site scripting (*http://en.wikipedia.org/wiki/Cross-site_scripting*) is a real risk, so make sure that all text to and from a plugin is encoded before it is displayed in a web page. This can be done with the $textutils.htmlEncode method, as shown in Example 2-5 and other examples.
- Cross-Site Request Forgery (XSRF, *http://en.wikipedia.org/wiki/Cross-site_request_is* forgery another type of risk that is reduced by adding a session token to all interactions with JIRA.

More specific information about these kinds of risks and how to control what users can do is available at *https://confluence.atlassian.com/display/ATL/Securing+your+Plugin*, *https://developer.atlassian.com/display/JIRADEV/Form+Token+Handling* and *https://developer.atlassian.com/display/SAL/Adding+WebSudo+Support+to+your+Plugin*.

Version One, Version Two and Version Three Plugins

As described at *https://developer.atlassian.com/display/JIRADEV/Differences+between+Plugins1+and+JIRA*, Plugins2's original "version one" plugin framework used Maven 1.x with a top-level project file named *project.xml* instead of *pom.xml*. The `.jar` file for these plugins was deployed to *atlassian-jira/WEB-INF/lib* instead of the current *jira.home/plugins/installed-plugins*.

Along with JIRA 4.0 came Maven 2 plugin projects and version two plugins. The difference is seen in the `plugins-version` attribute of the `atlassian-plugin` element at the top of the *atlassian-plugin.xml* file. If this attribute is not present, then the plugin is a version one plugin.

The newer version two plugins use the OSGI framework to control the order in which different plugins start and stop, and as of JIRA 4.4 can be updated without restarting JIRA, in most cases. The other main difference for plugin developers between the two types of plugins is that version two plugins are loaded in their own Java class loader, which means that by default they can only access some of the core JIRA classes. There are a number of ways to work with this restriction documented at *https://developer.atlassian.com/display/DOCS/Plugin+and+Gadget+Gotchas*.

Unless you've got a very good reason not to, you should write any new JIRA plugin as a version two plugin.

Version three plugins will likely involve a `.jar` file that contains the usual files for local execution, and also files that can be executed in a remote *Platform as a Service* service such as Heroku or Google App Engine. Allowing remote execution means that JIRA instances in Atlassian's cloud-based OnDemand service can connect to the remote server to add new functionality, instead of changing installed files.

JIRA Development Mode

JIRA can be started up in a development mode that can make some parts of developing plugins a little easier. If you add `-Djira.dev.mode=true` to the JVM parameters in *bin/setenv.sh*, then JIRA does the following.

- Velocity template files and internationalization properties files outside plugins are reloaded when used.
- No email is read or sent.
- JavaScript files are not compressed which makes them easier to read.
- Jelly scripts are enabled.
- Some dashboard caching is not used.

- The jira.home directory can be a relative directory.

Using a Debugger with JIRA

Some problems during development need the precision that a debugger offers. Understanding the sequence of method calls is certainly easier with a debugger.

The easiest way to configure JIRA for use with a debugger is to use the SDK command *atlas-debug* to start up a new instance of JIRA, as documented at *https://developer.atlassian.com/display/DOCS/atlas-debug*. If you're using an IDE, you can then connect to JIRA as described at *https://developer.atlassian.com/display/DOCS/Creating+a+remote+debug+target*.

To connect a debugger to an existing instance of JIRA, you have to add certain JVM flags to JIRA. This is typically done by adding the following lines to the JIRA startup script in *bin/setenv.sh*.

```
JAVA_OPTS="-Xrunjdwp:transport=dt_socket,address=8000,server=y,suspend=n $JAVA_OPTS"
JAVA_OPTS="-Xdebug $JAVA_OPTS"
```

Once JIRA has been restarted, then you can connect the debugger to it, on port 8000 in this case. The simplest command to do this is jdb -attach localhost:8080, but there are plenty of other graphical debuggers with more features available. A stand-alone debugger that I like is *JDebugTool* from *http://www.debugtools.If/*. com you're using an IDE such as Eclipse, then you probably already have a graphical debugger available as part of the IDE.

For information about attaching to your tests using a debugger, see *http://maven.apache.org/plugins/maven-surefire-plugin/examples/debugging.html*.

Further Reading

There's a large collection of JIRA plugin development steps and other tips in Jobin Kuruvilla's JIRA Development Cookbook (*http://www.packtpub.com/jira-to-develop-customize-plugins-program-workflows-cookbook/book*). Jobin is also the author of the j-tricks blogs that are mentioned throughout this book.

About the Author

Matt Doar is based in San Jose, CA where he works with CustomWare, a professional services company that is also Atlassian's oldest and largest Platinum Expert organization. He has been helping other people with JIRA for over seven years and is the author of a number of JIRA plugins as part of the wider Atlassian development community. He also wrote Practical JIRA Plugins (O'Reilly) and Practical Development Environments (O'Reilly), which described the basics of software tools—version control, build tools, testing, issue trackers, and automation. He has also held some sort of dubious record for the most bugs submitted about JIRA by a non-Atlassian. Before JIRA entered his world, Matt was a developer and then a software toolsmith at various networking companies. Before all that, he completed his B.A. and Ph.D. in Computer Networking at the University of Cambridge Computer Laboratory and St. John's College, Cambridge.

Colophon

The animal on the cover of *Practical JIRA Plugins* is a king eider duck (*Somateria spedahilis*).

The cover image is from Johnson's Natural History. The cover font is Adobe ITC Garamond. The text font is Linotype Birka; the heading font is Adobe Myriad Condensed; and the code font is LucasFont's TheSansMonoCondensed.

Get even more for your money.

Join the O'Reilly Community, and register the O'Reilly books you own. It's free, and you'll get:

- $4.99 ebook upgrade offer
- 40% upgrade offer on O'Reilly print books
- Membership discounts on books and events
- Free lifetime updates to ebooks and videos
- Multiple ebook formats, DRM FREE
- Participation in the O'Reilly community
- Newsletters
- Account management
- 100% Satisfaction Guarantee

Signing up is easy:

1. **Go to: oreilly.com/go/register**
2. **Create an O'Reilly login.**
3. **Provide your address.**
4. **Register your books.**

Note: English-language books only

To order books online:
oreilly.com/store

For questions about products or an order:
orders@oreilly.com

To sign up to get topic-specific email announcements and/or news about upcoming books, conferences, special offers, and new technologies:
elists@oreilly.com

For technical questions about book content:
booktech@oreilly.com

To submit new book proposals to our editors:
proposals@oreilly.com

O'Reilly books are available in multiple DRM-free ebook formats. For more information:
oreilly.com/ebooks

O'REILLY®

Spreading the knowledge of innovators   oreilly.com